Escape Into Color

ADULT COLORING BOOK

THUY COOK

Copyright © 2017 by Thuy Cook

All rights reserved. No part of this publication may be reproduced, distributed, or transmitted in any form or by any means, including photocopying, recording, or other electronic or mechanical methods, without the prior written permission of the publisher.

ISBN-13: 978-1979263351
ISBN-10: 1979263353

For information about custom editions, special sales, and premium and corporate purchases, please email thuy.cook@gmail.com.

Printed in the United States of America

This book belongs to
....

For Aria

Introduction

Free your creativity as you explore Escape Into Color. This coloring book offers an escape to a world of inspiration and artistic fulfilment. From calming flora to curious creatures, each inky drawing is waiting your colorful creations to bring to life.

Tips for Coloring:

- 🐝 Use the color palette test page at the back of this book to test your pencils and pens.

- 🐝 Use a few scrap pieces of paper between pages in case it bleeds through to the next sheet.

- 🐝 Add dark colors to intensity shading.

- 🐝 Shade light colors over dark to blend.

- 🐝 Share your creations with friends on social media with the hashtag #escapeintocolor.

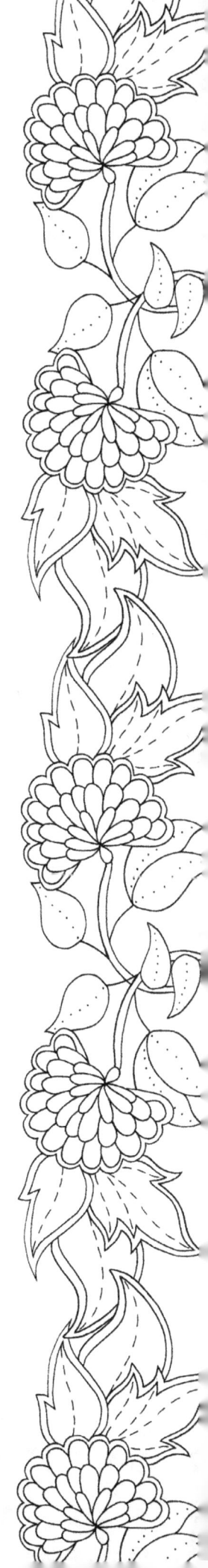

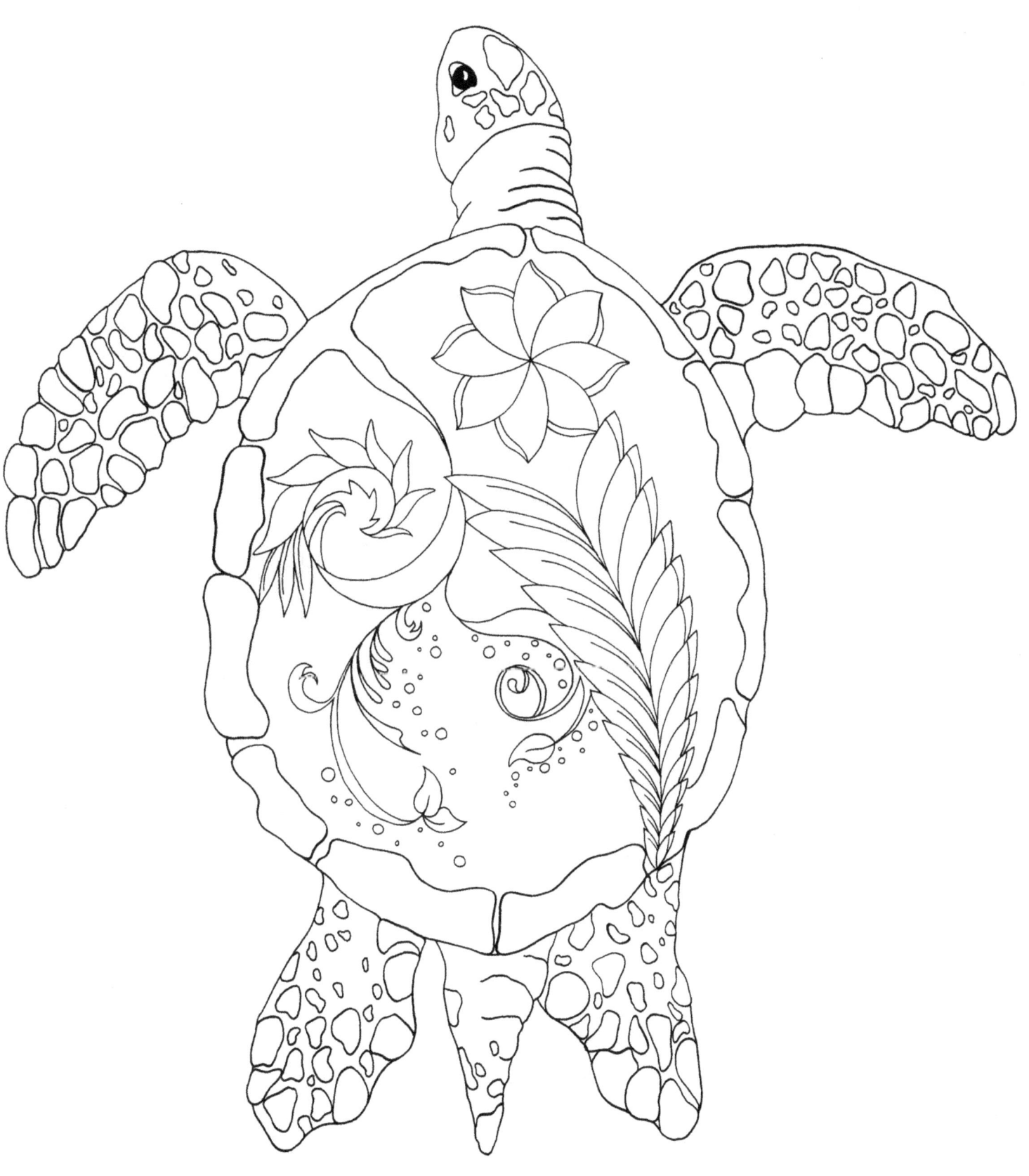

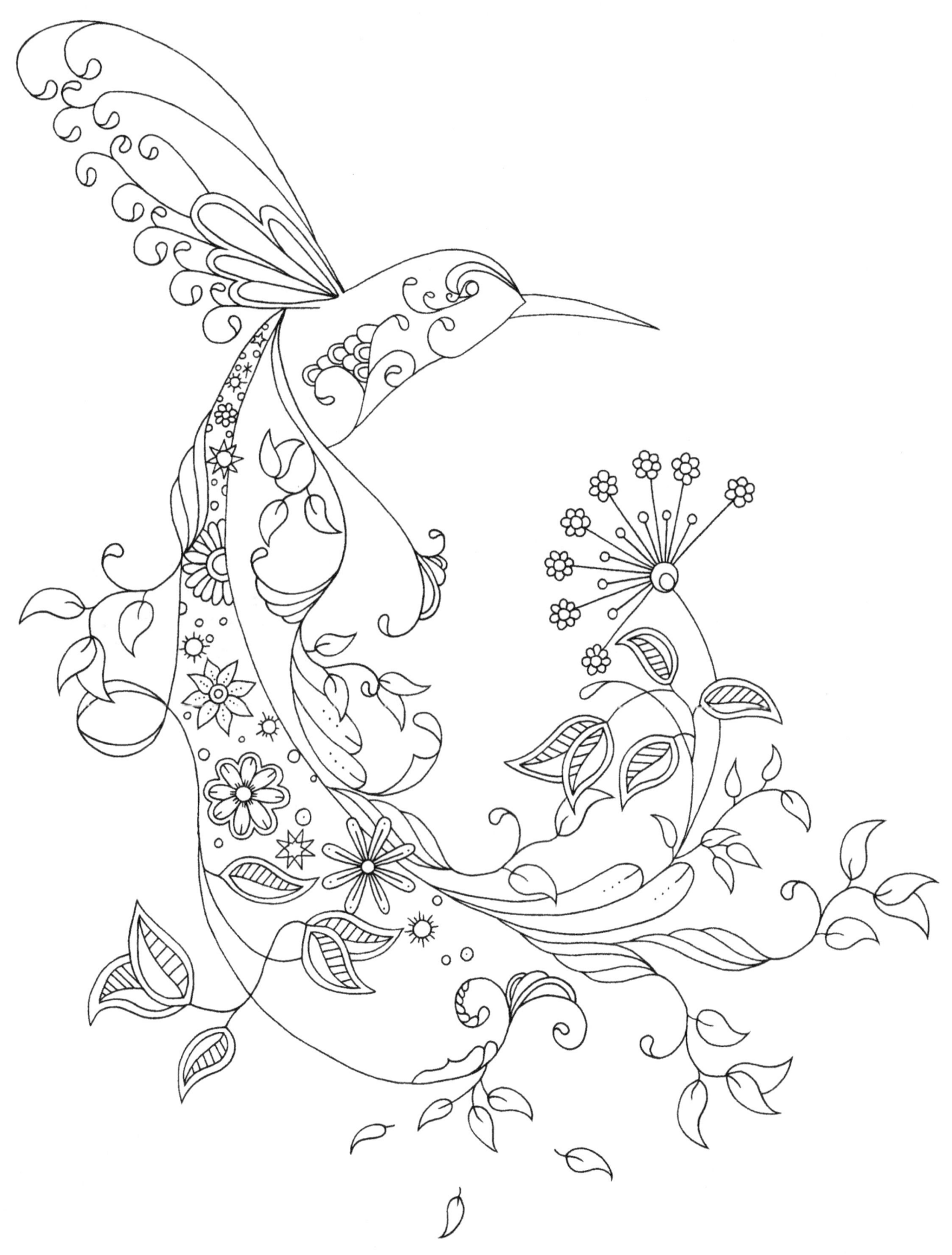

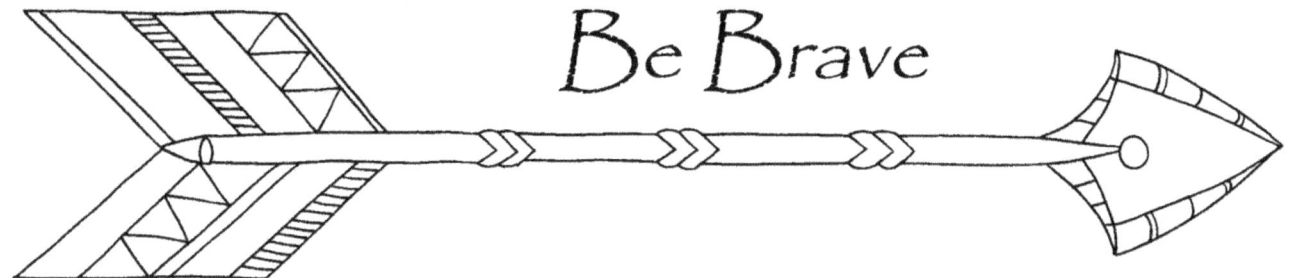
Be Brave

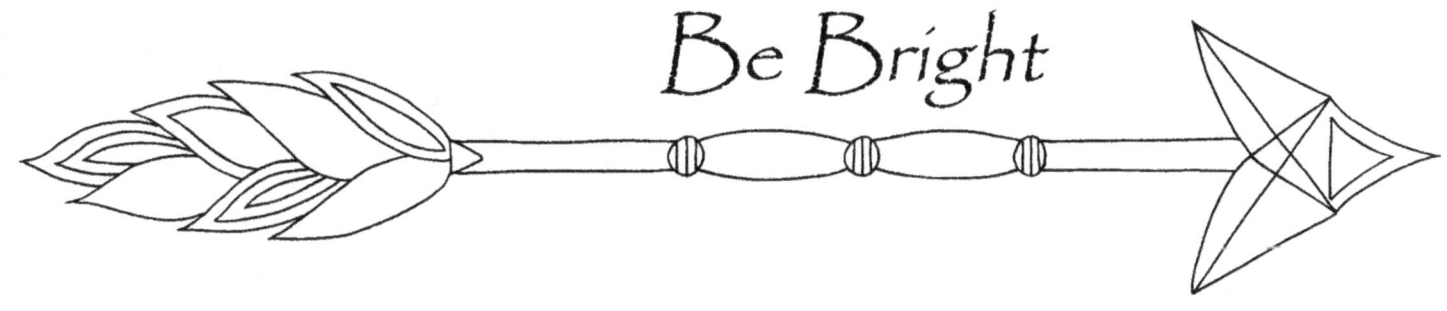
Be Bright

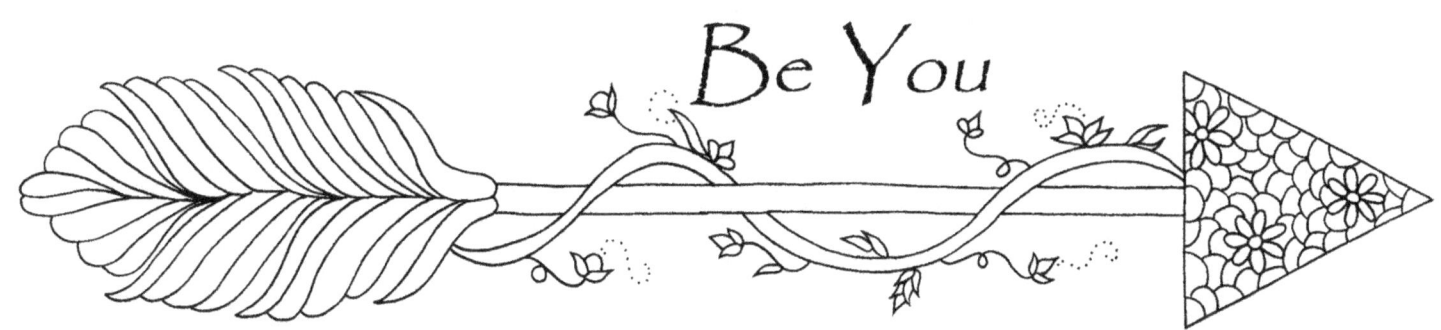
Be You

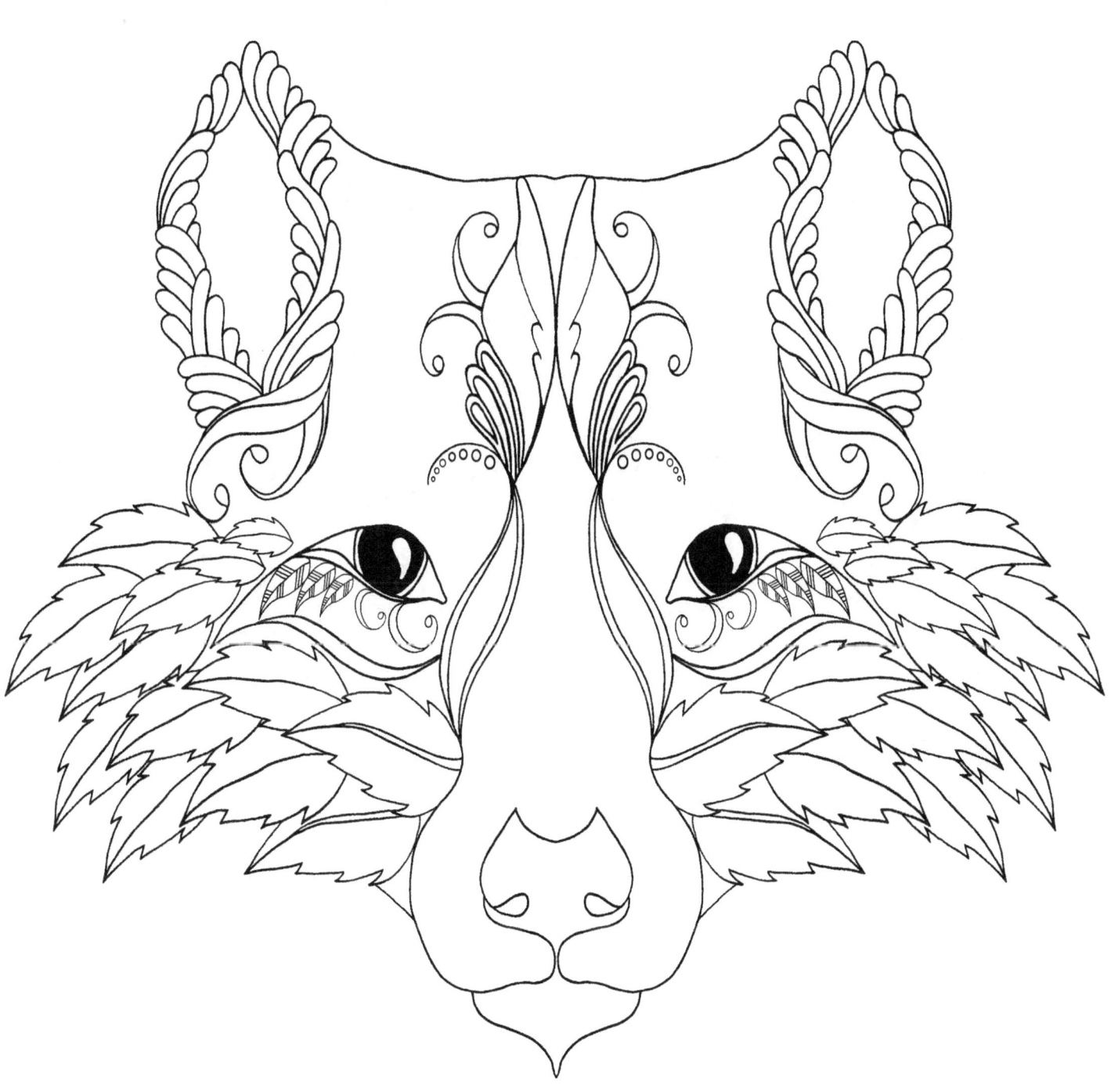

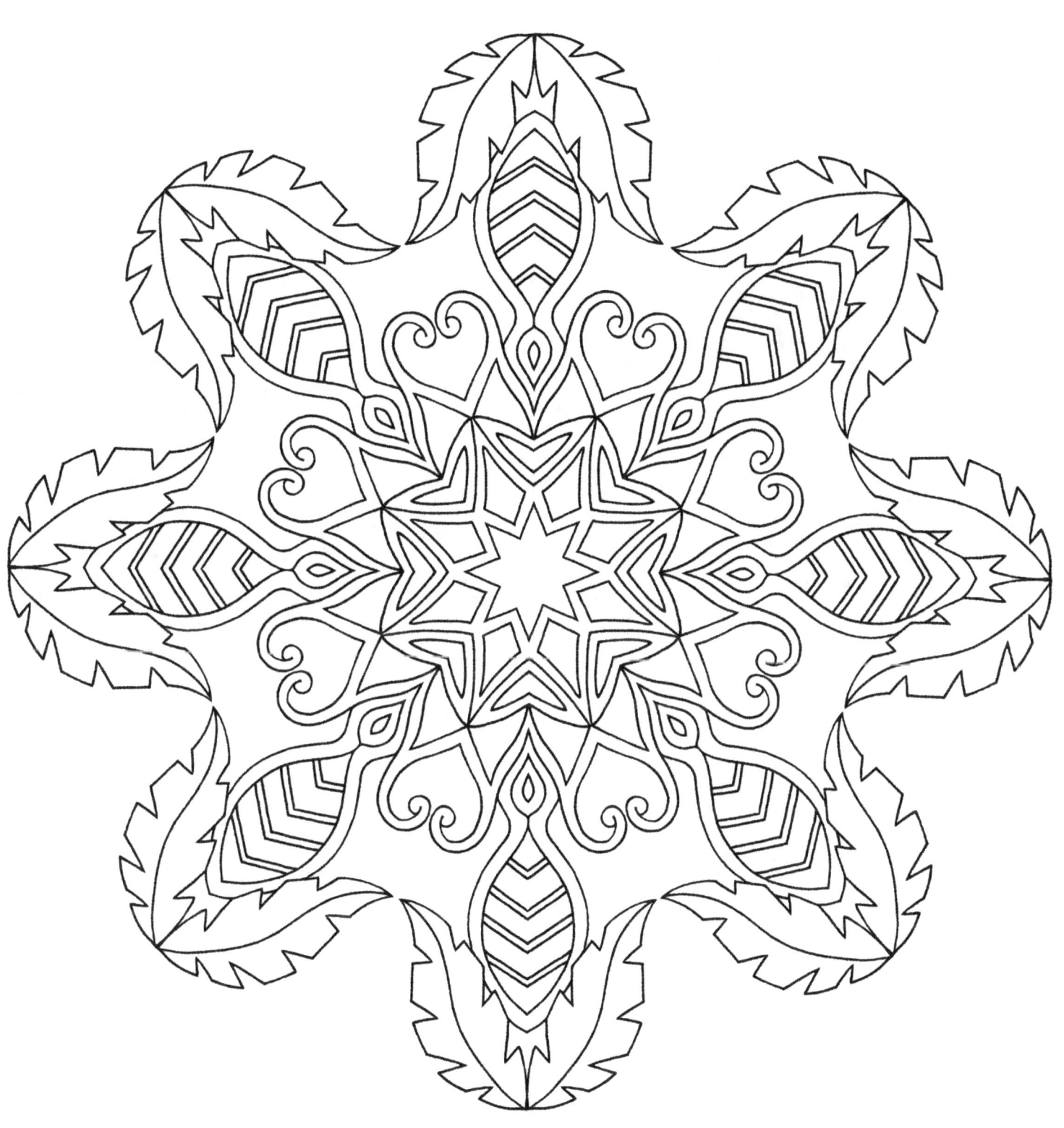

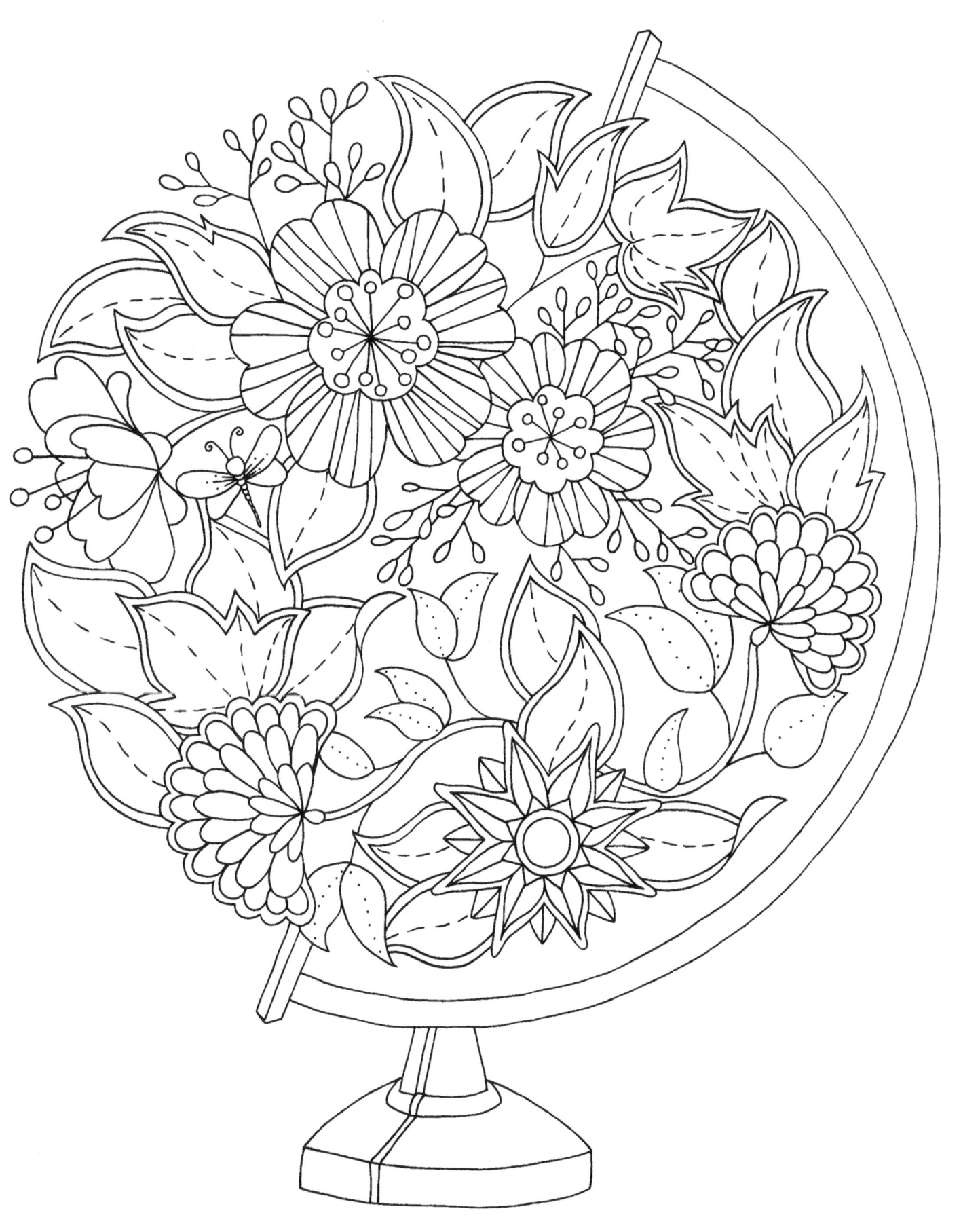

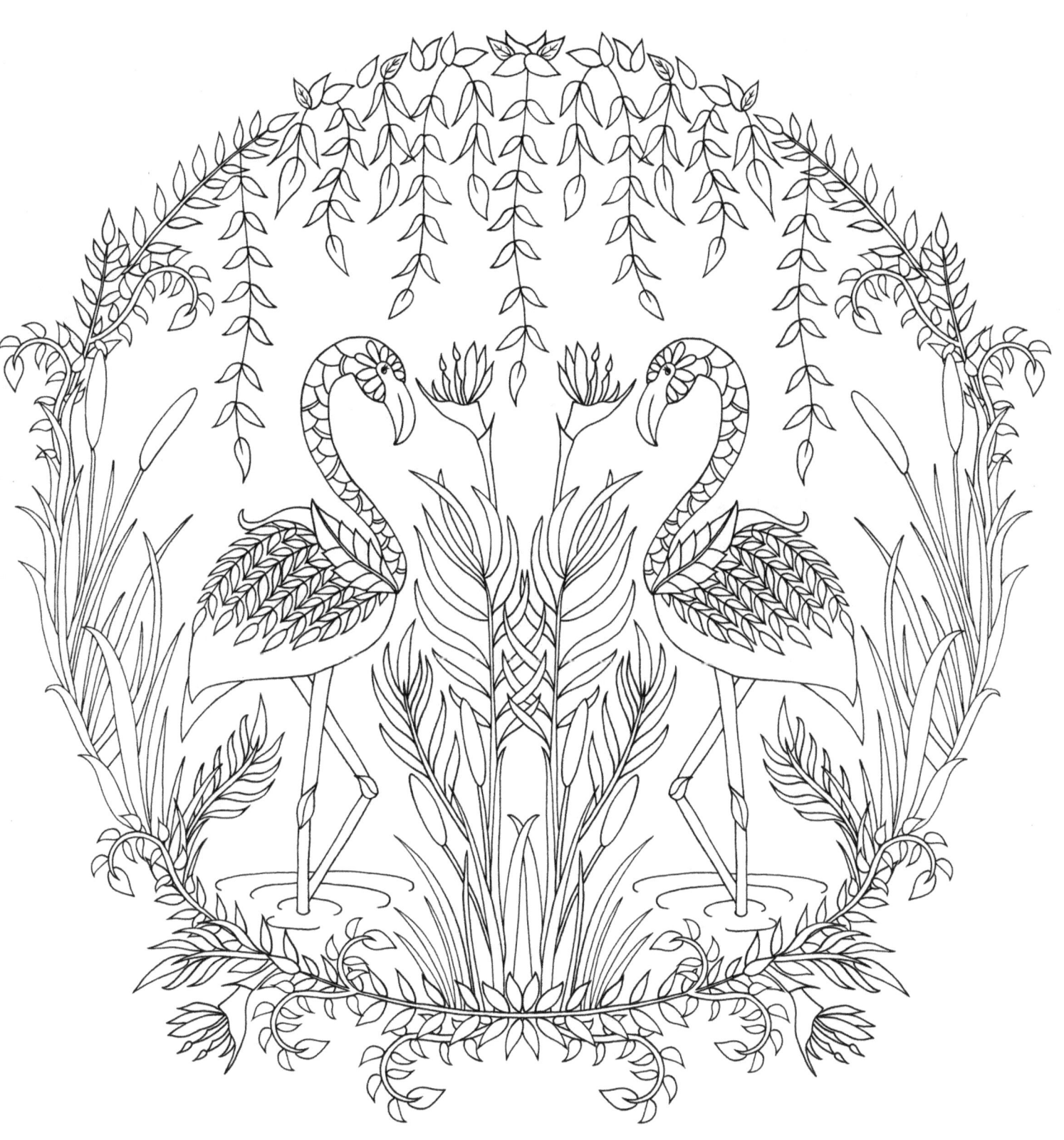

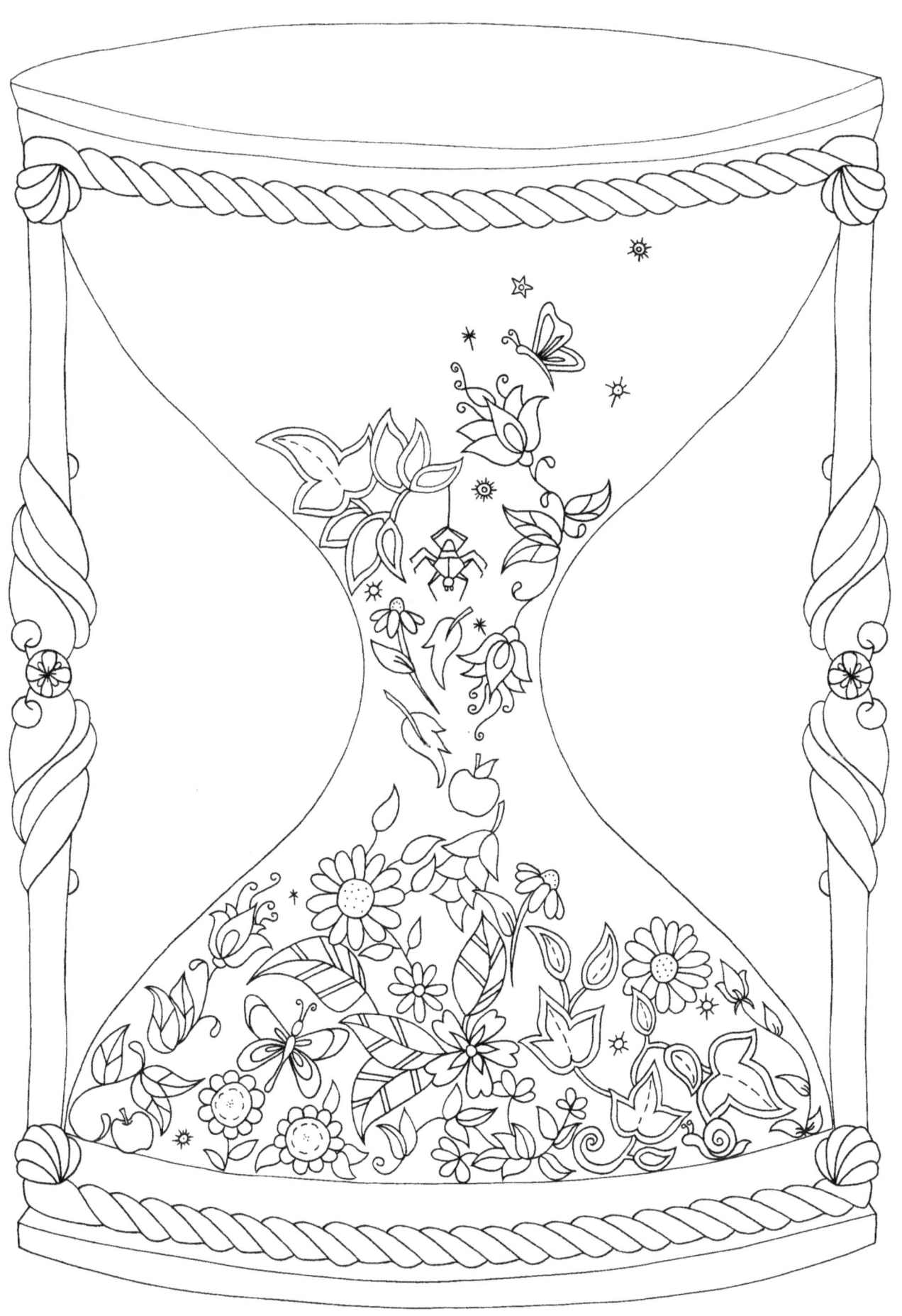

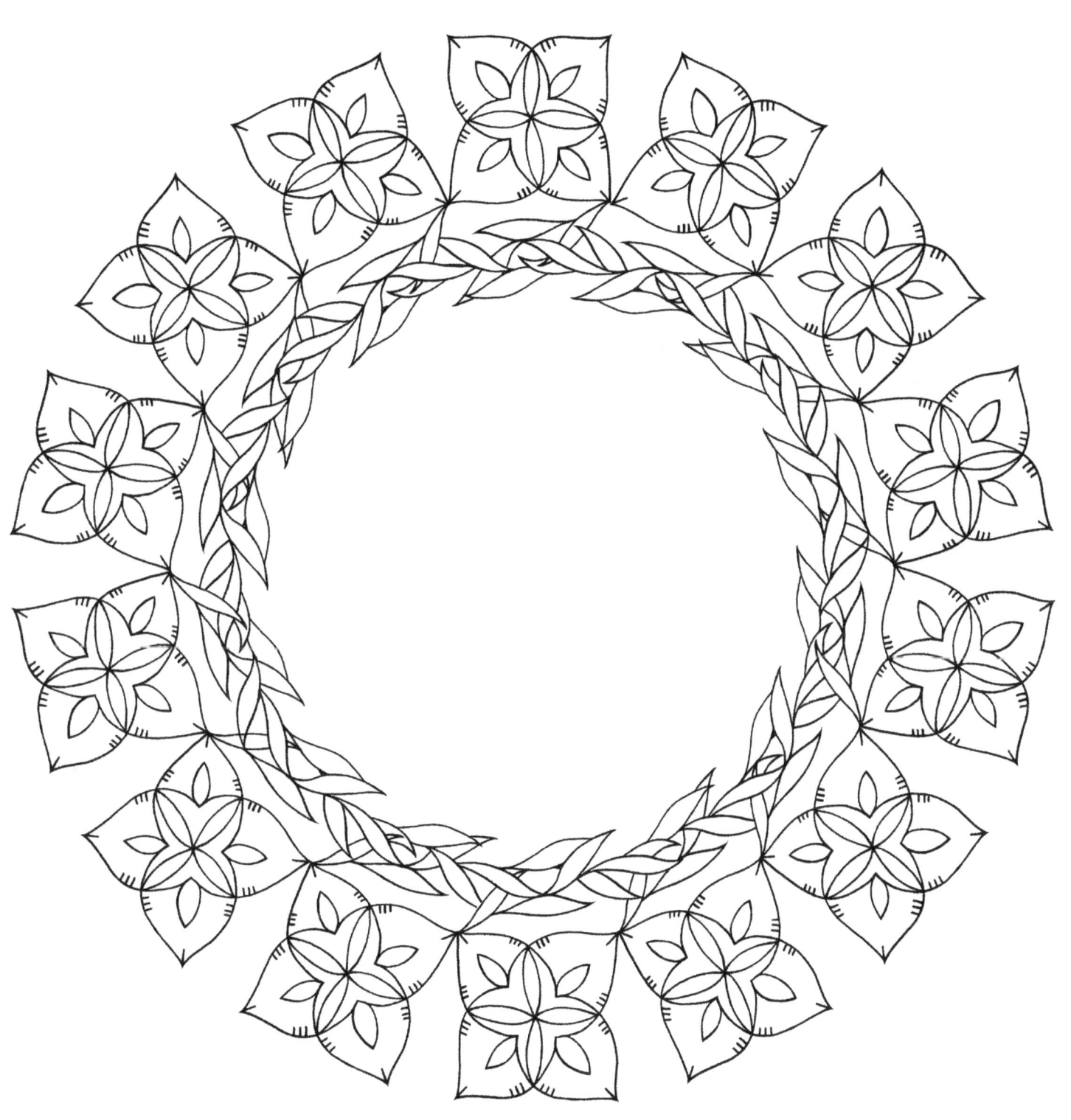

Fill the butterflies with detail.

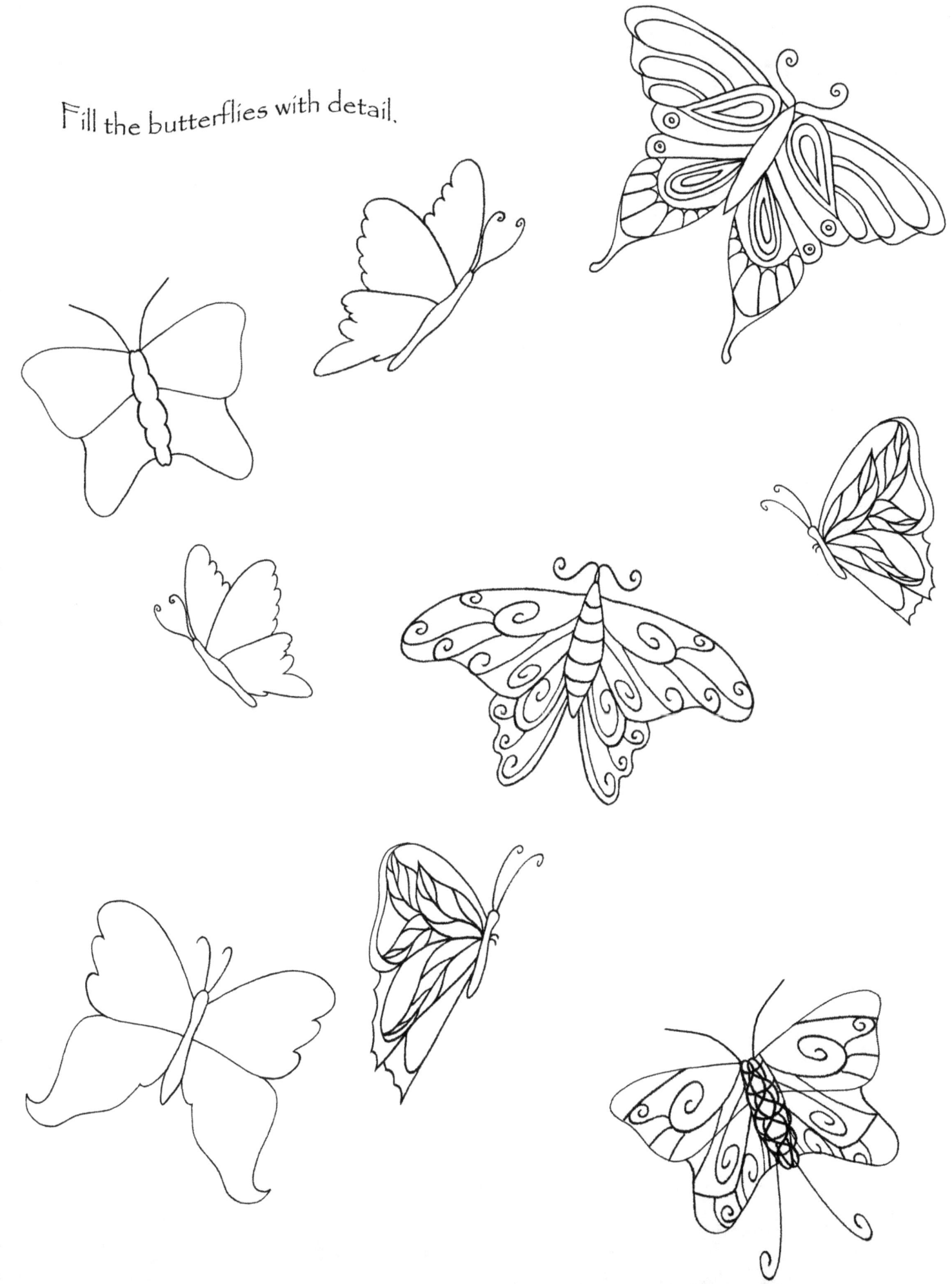

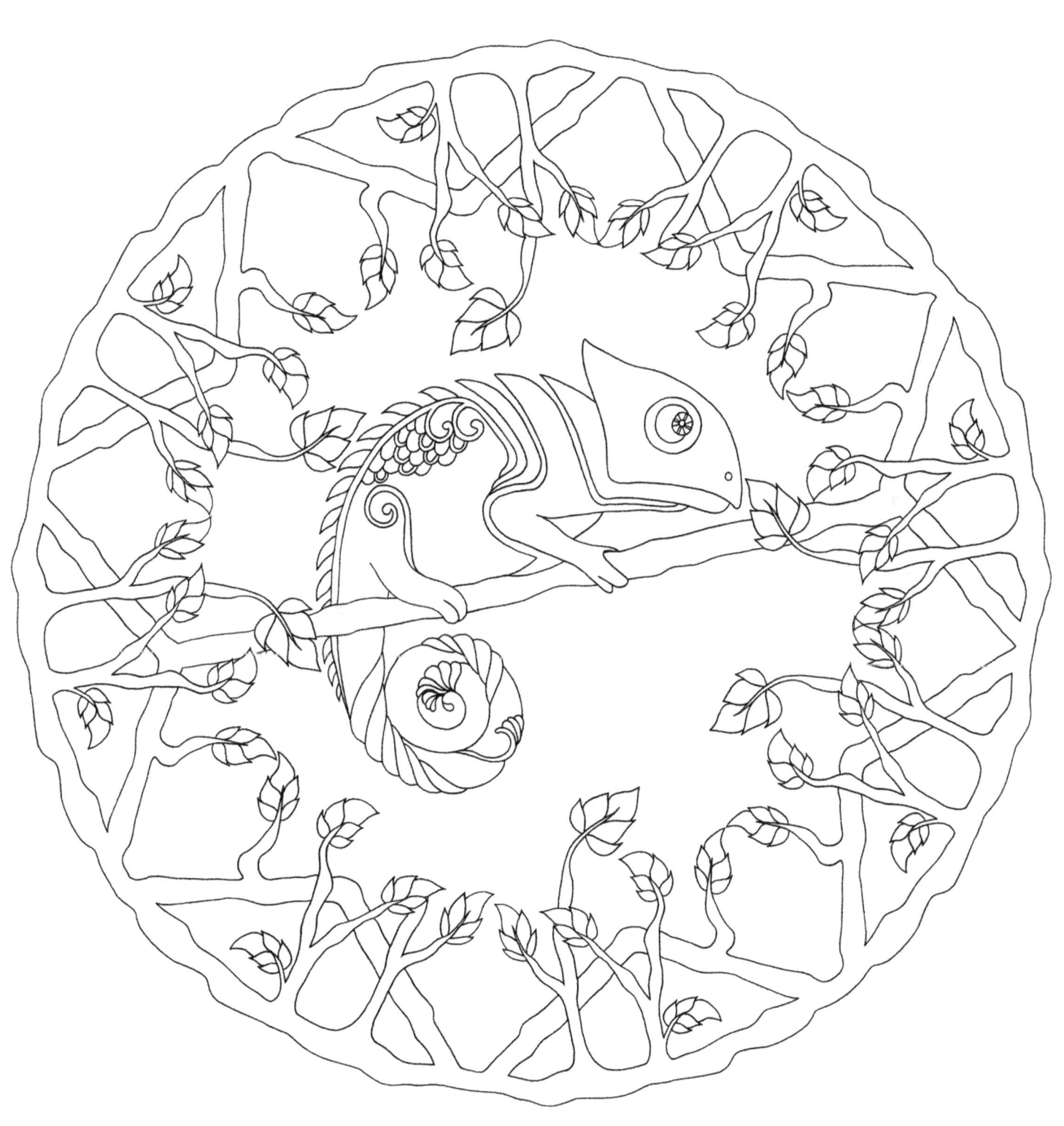

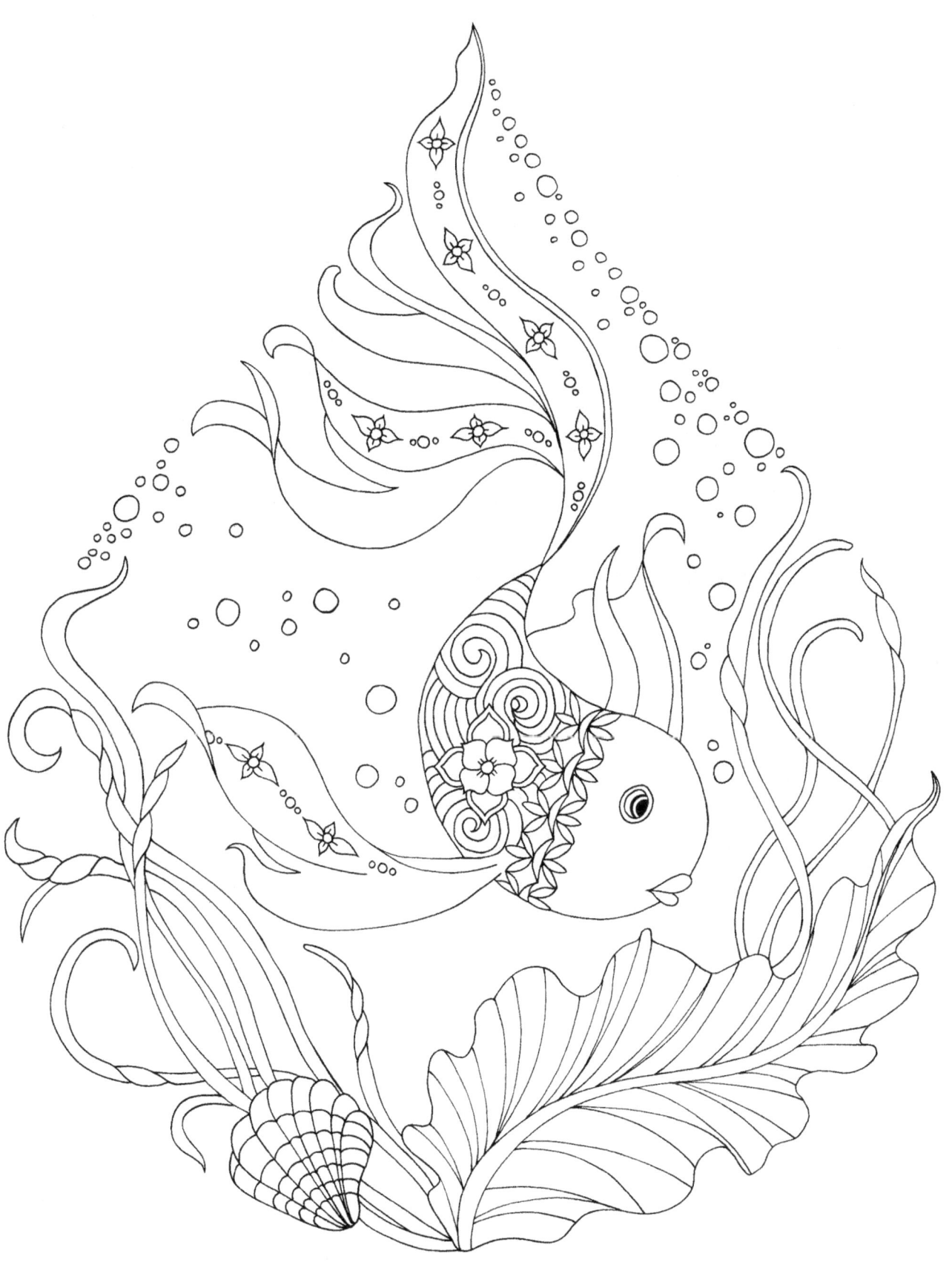

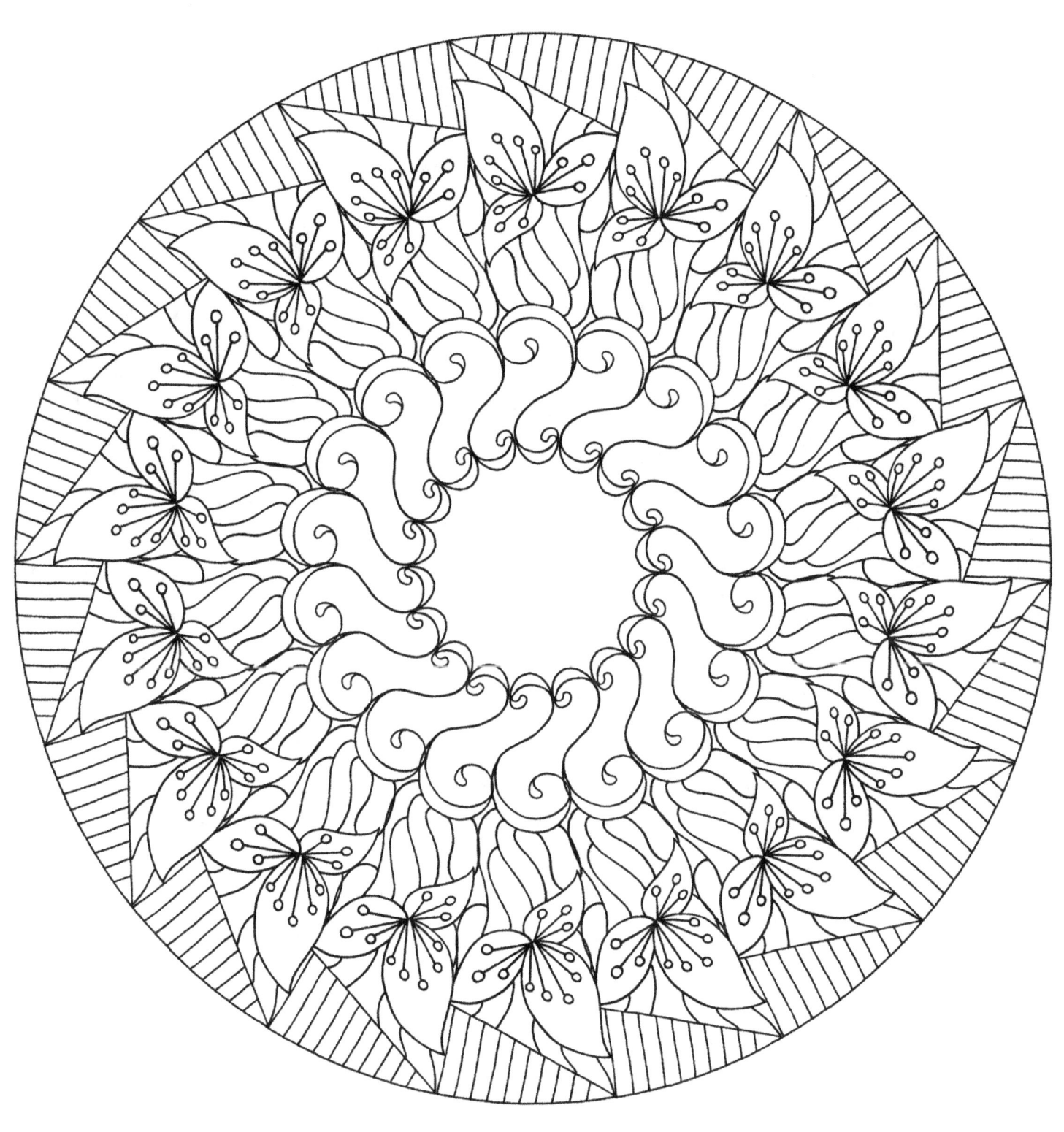

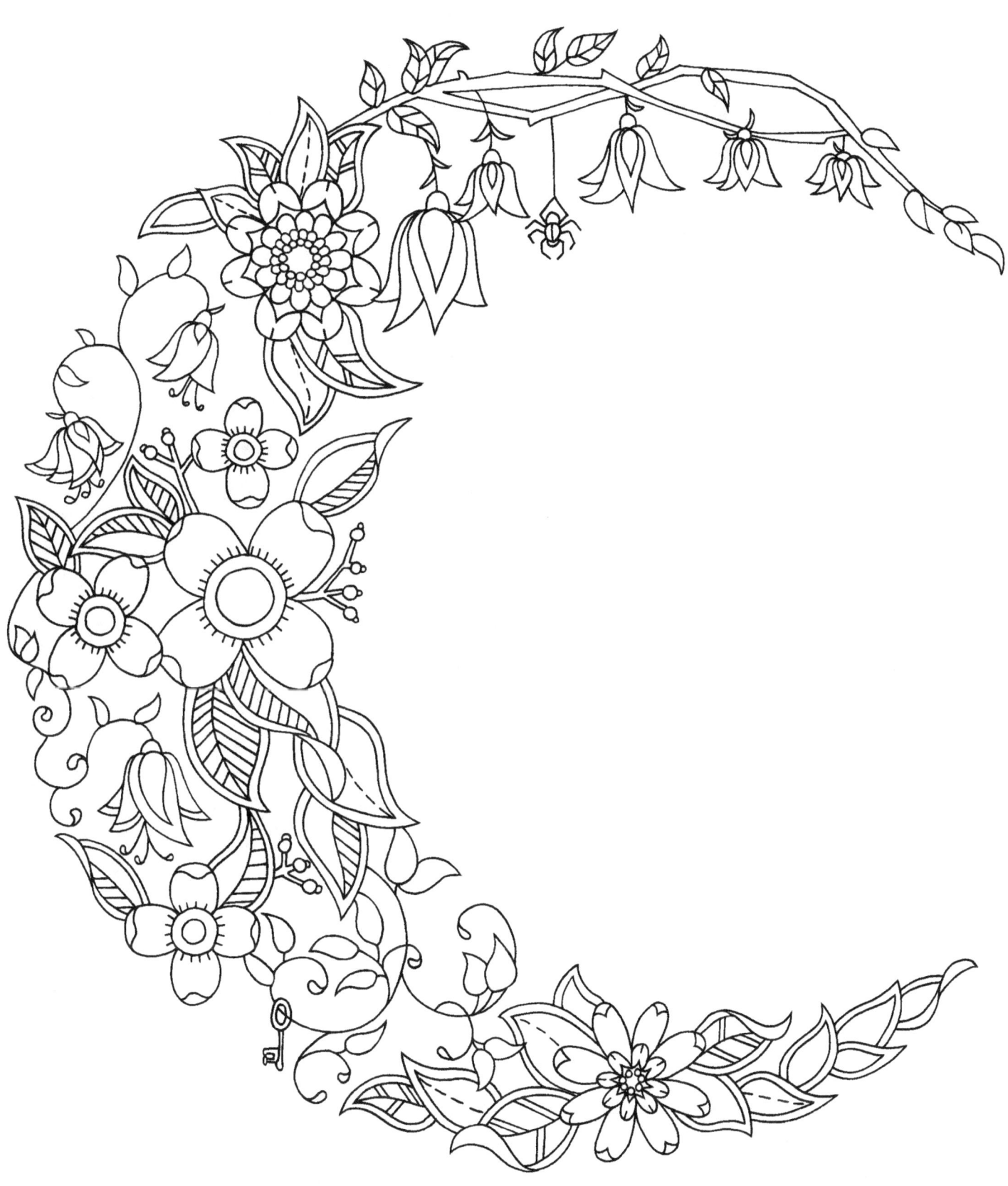

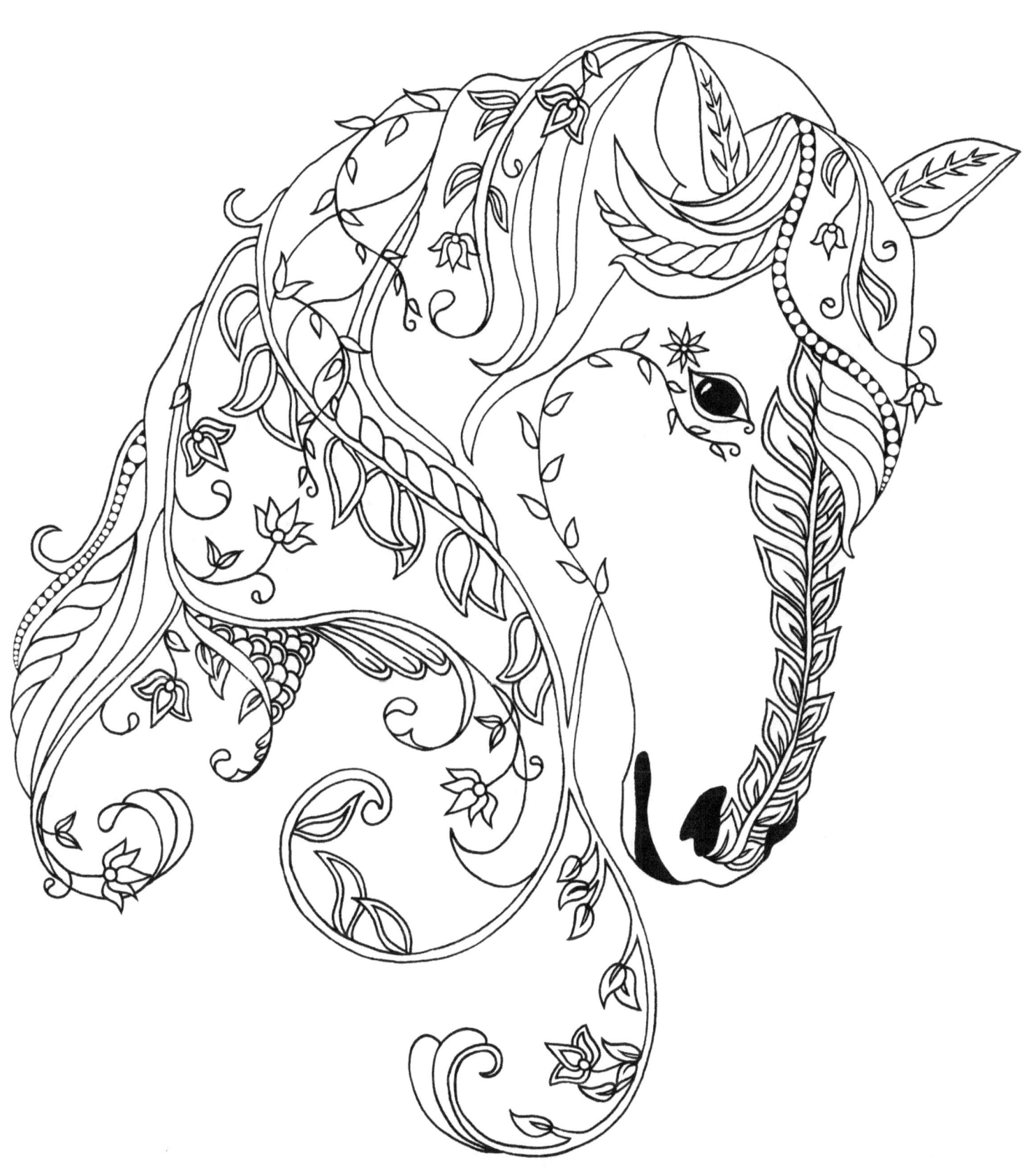

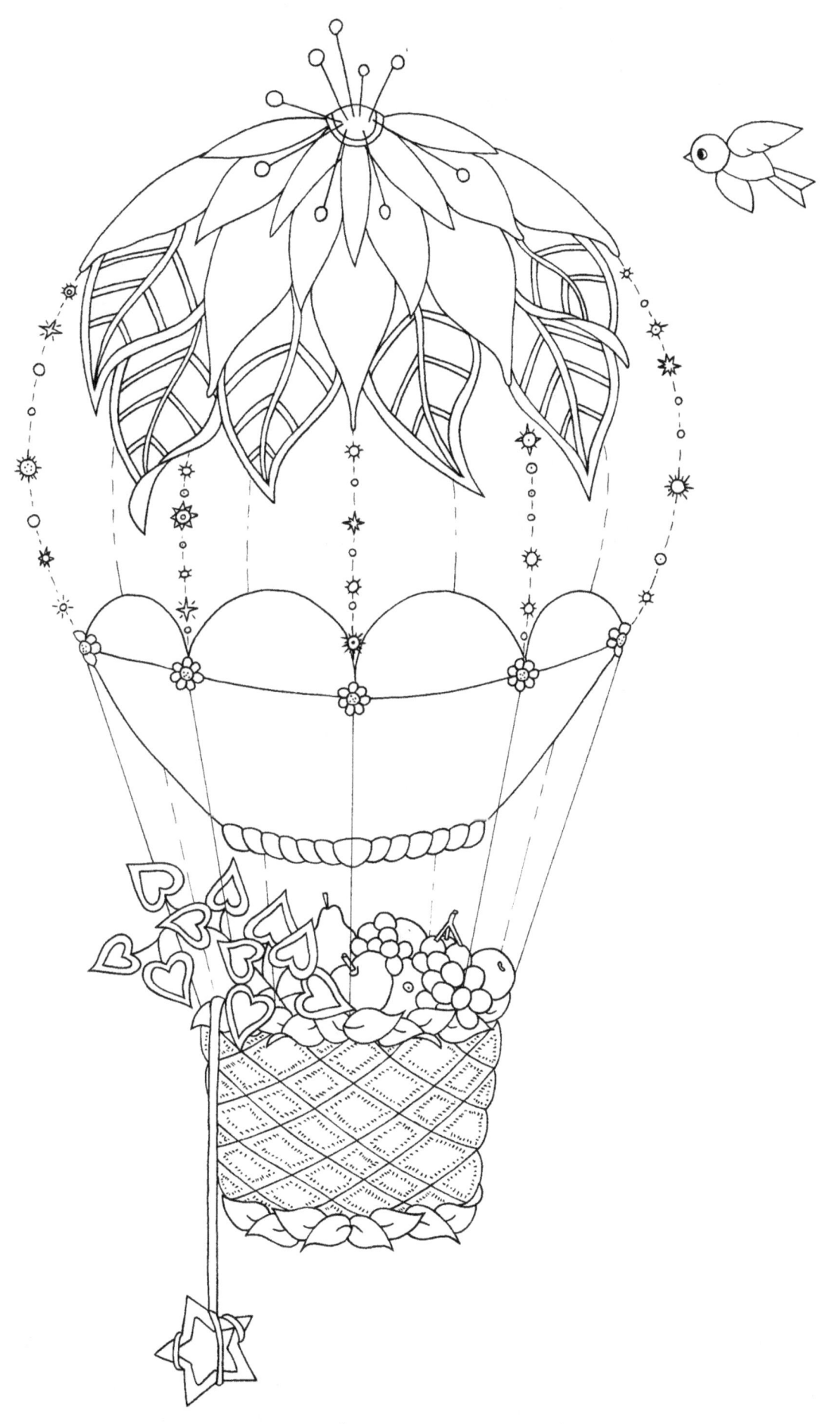

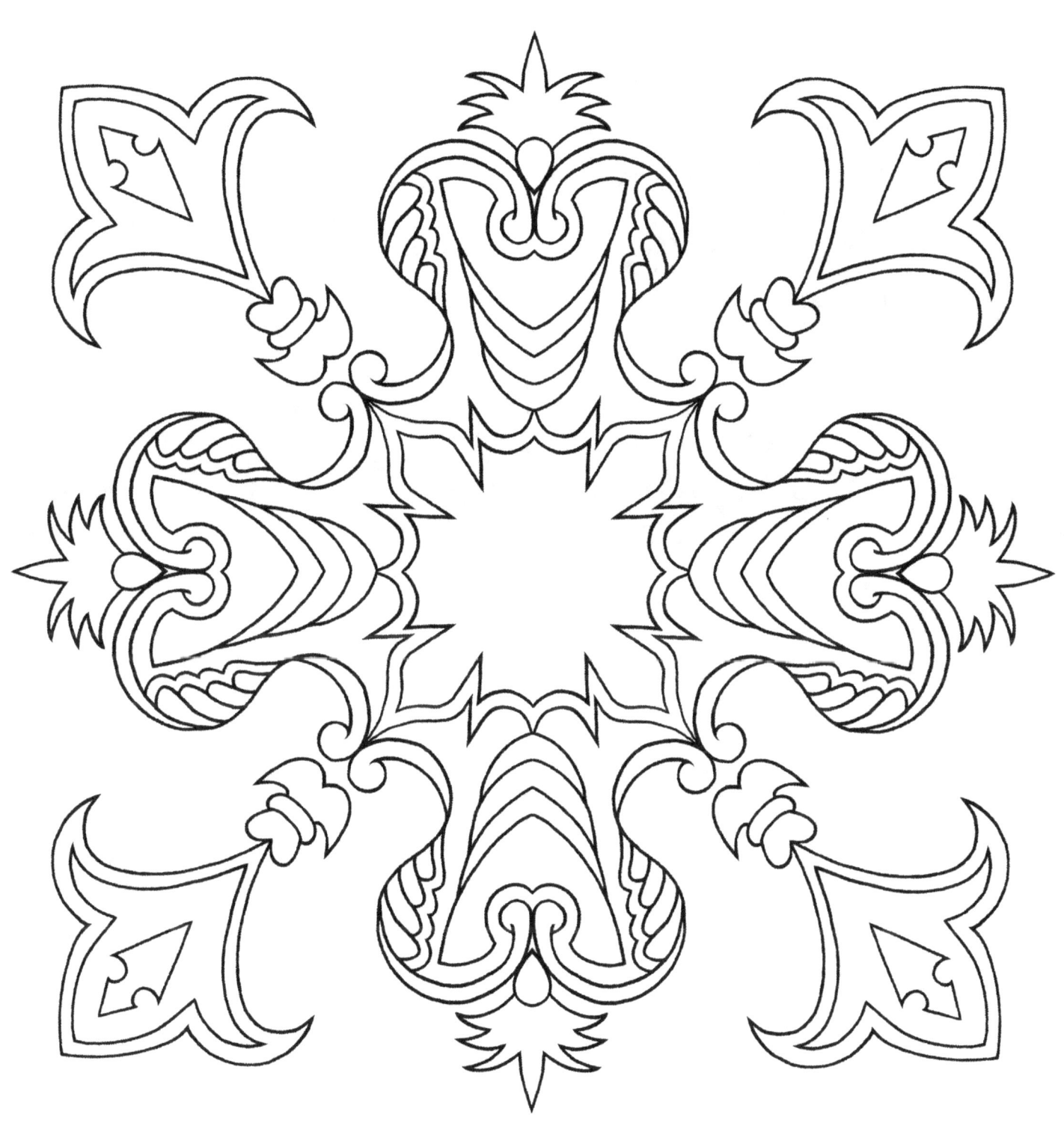

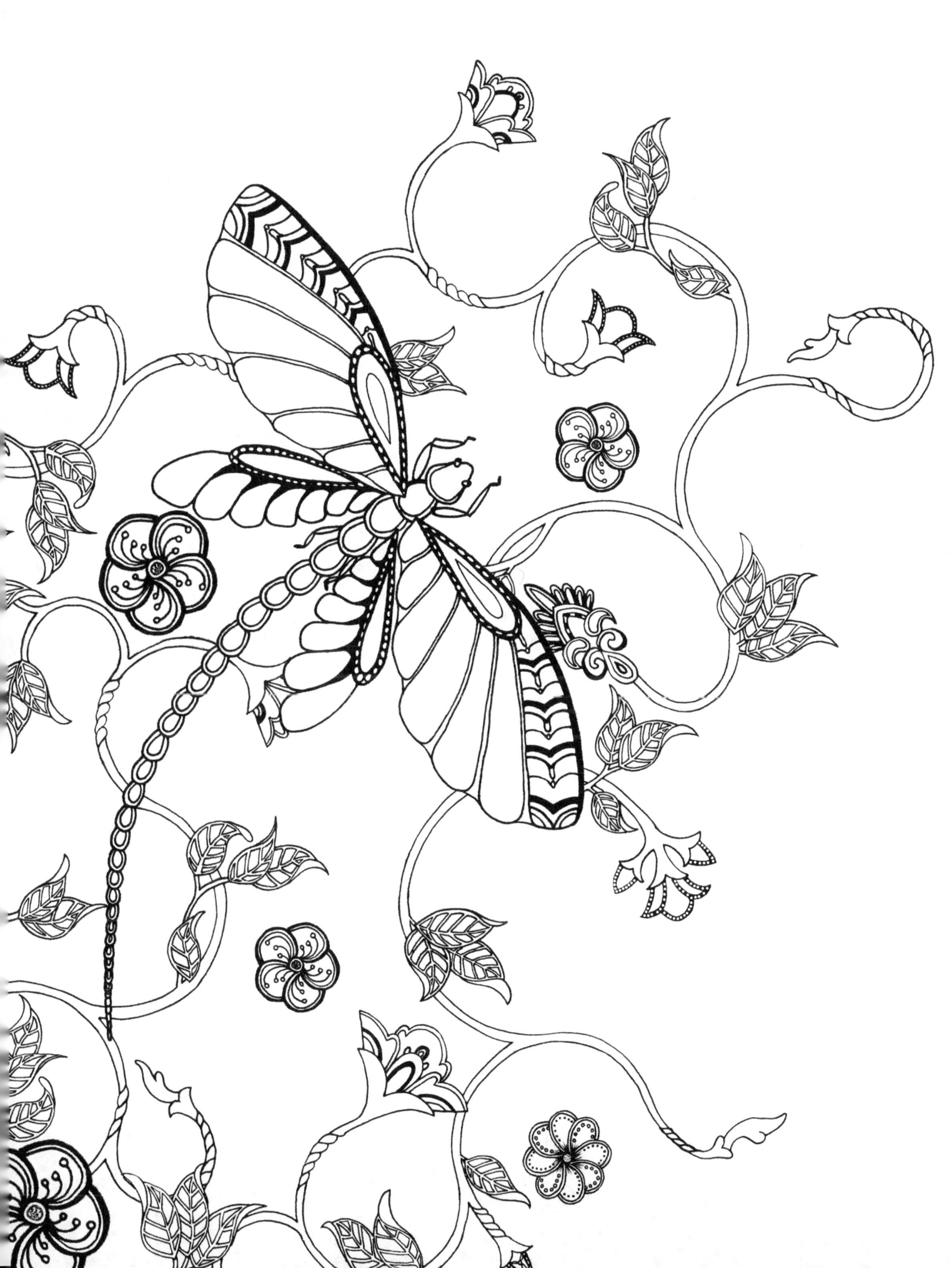

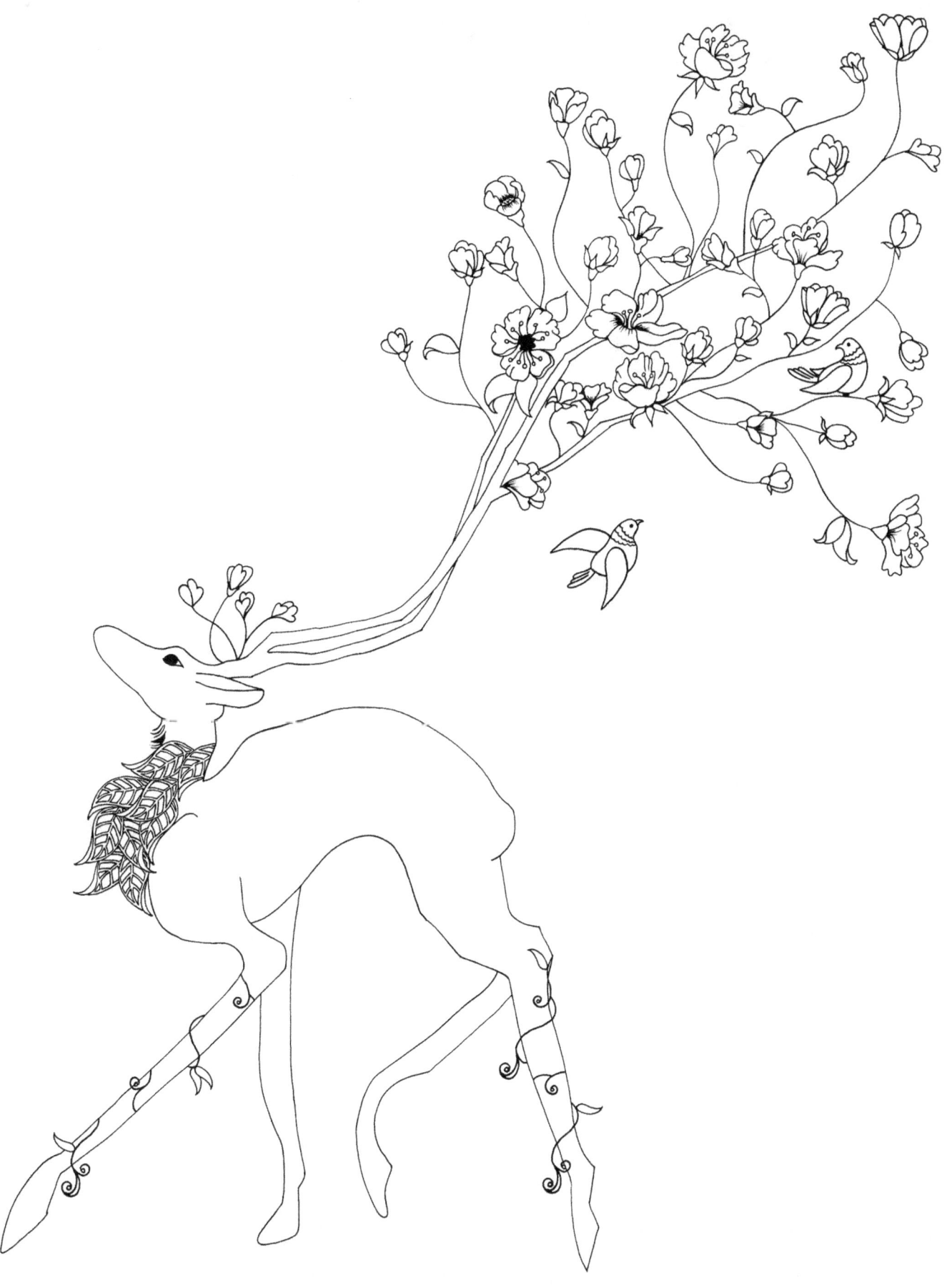

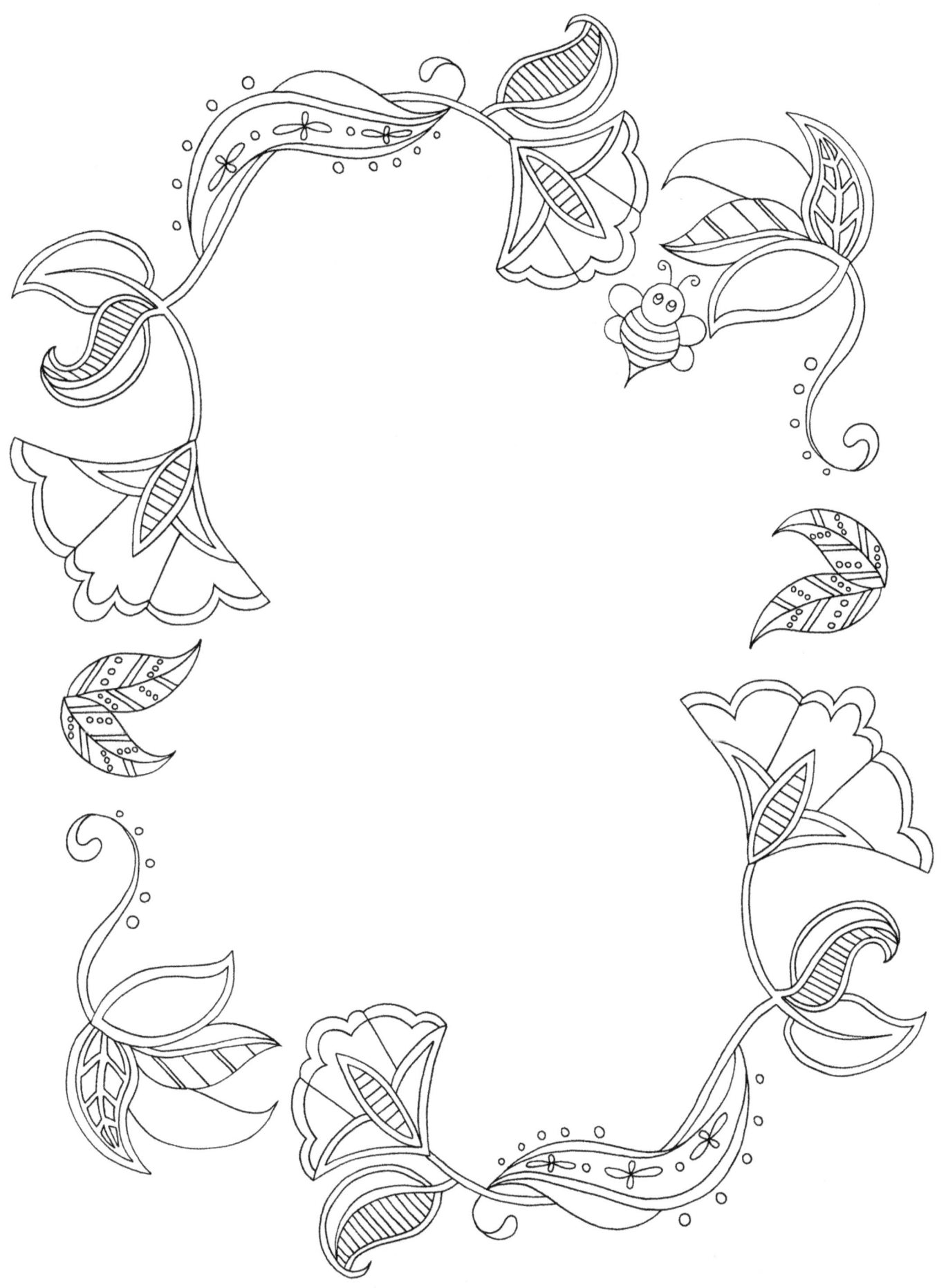

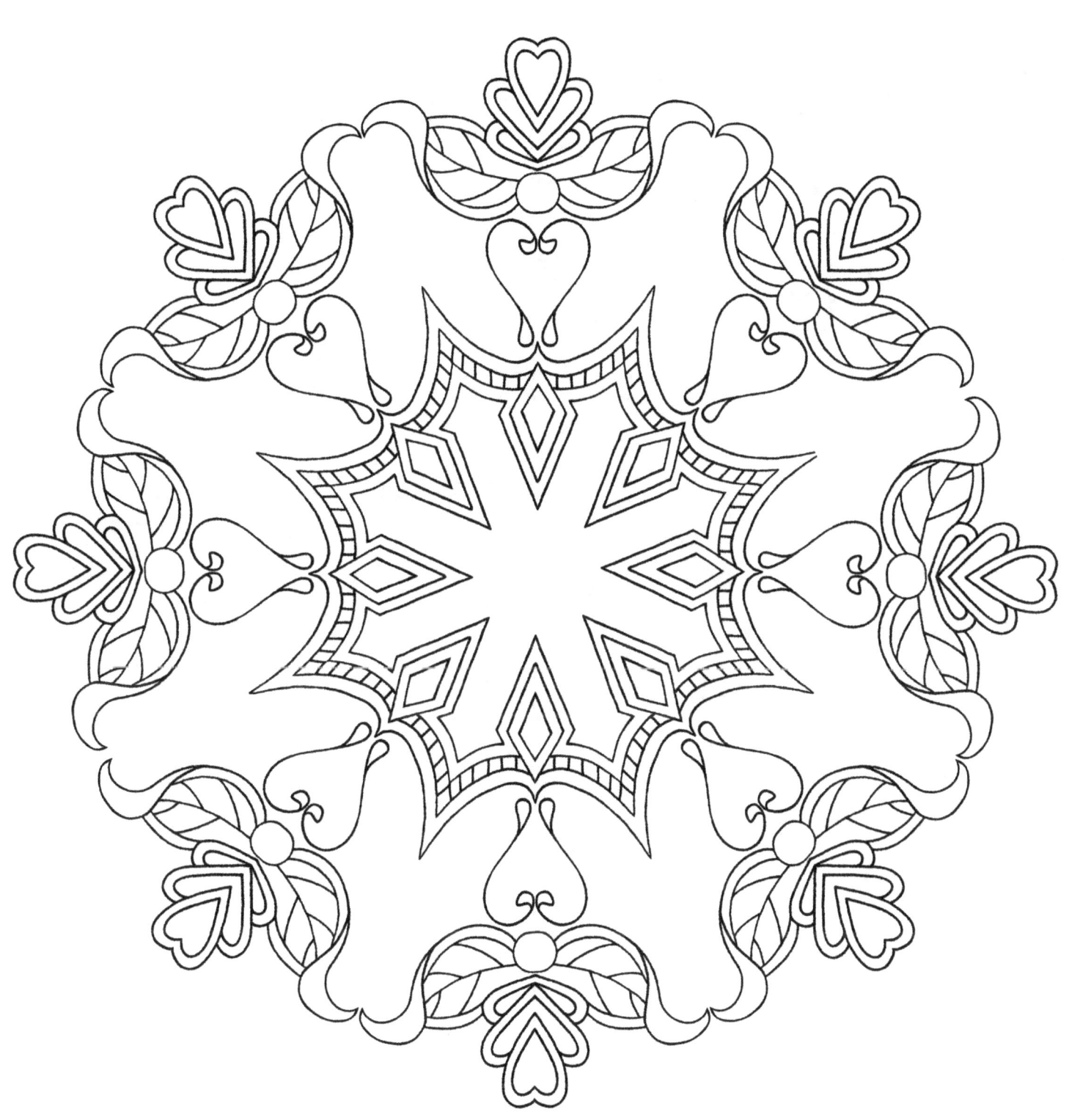

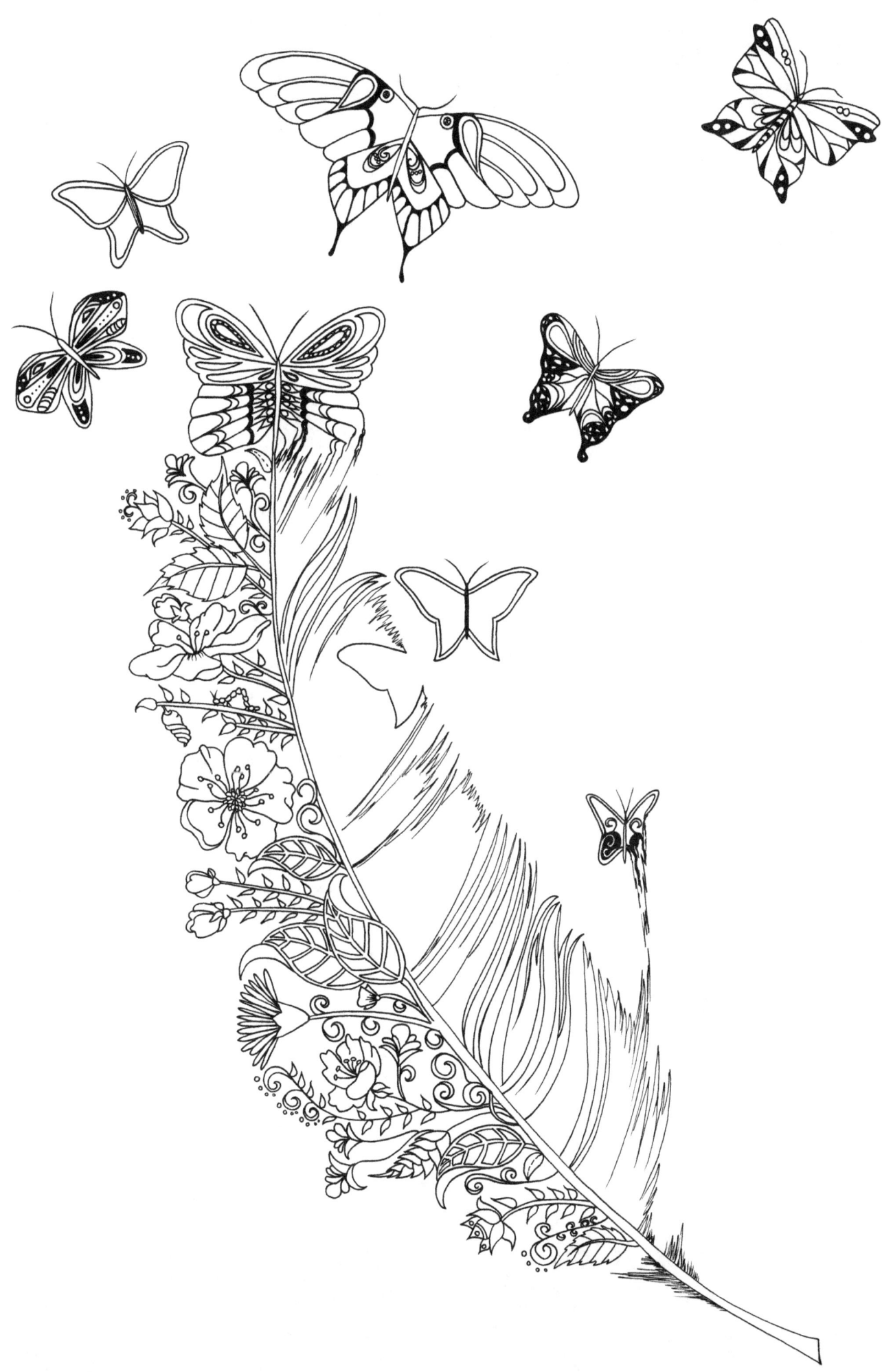

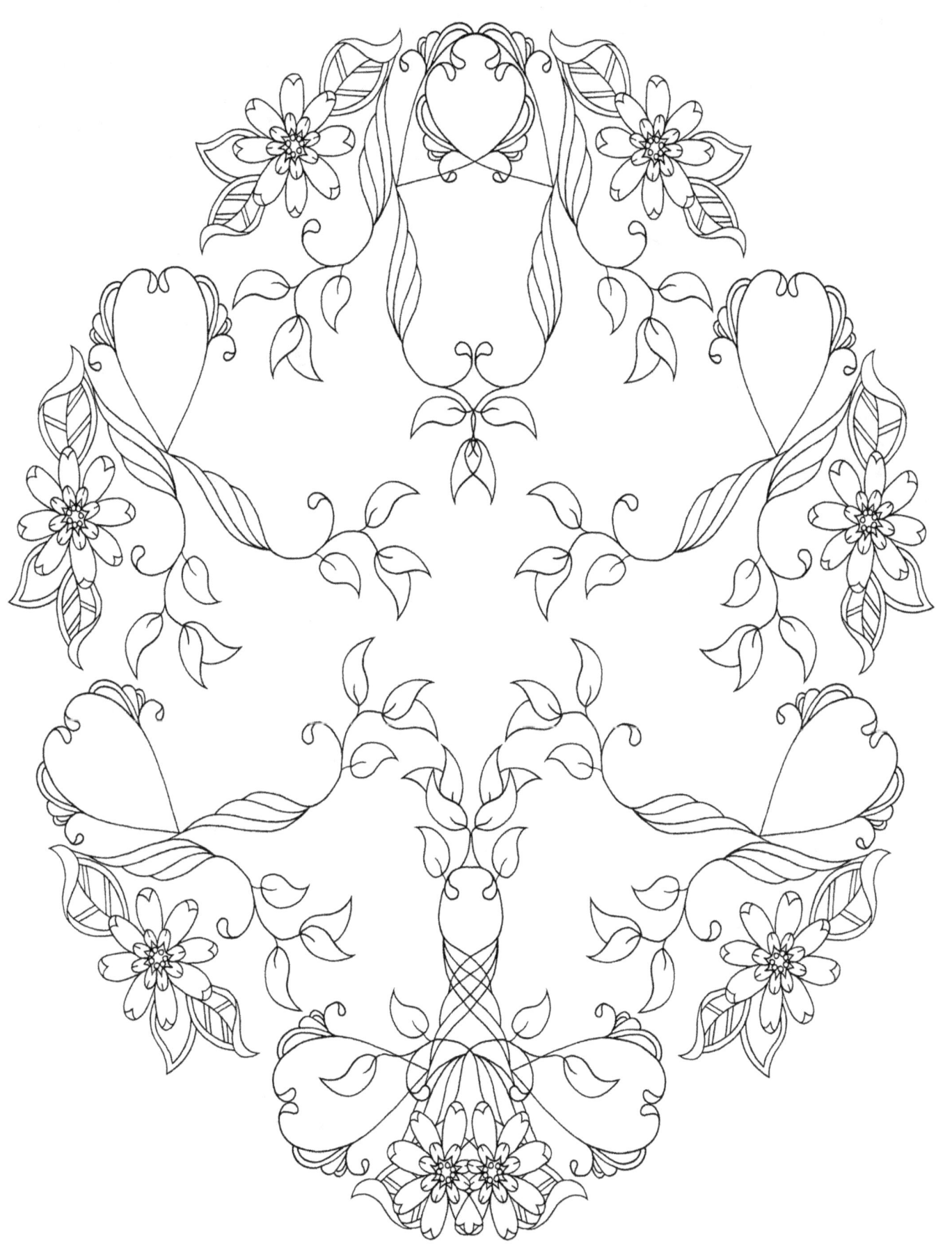

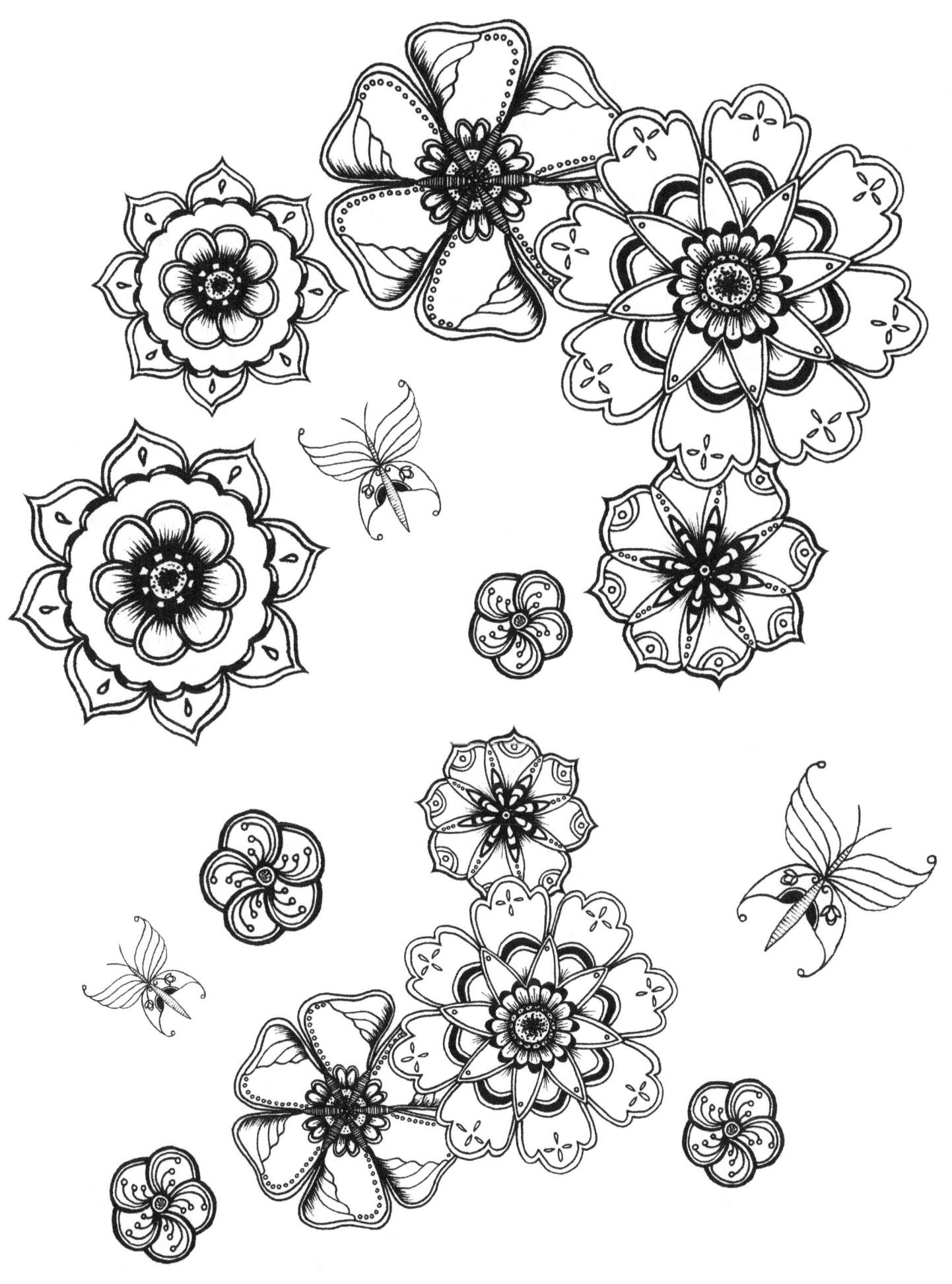

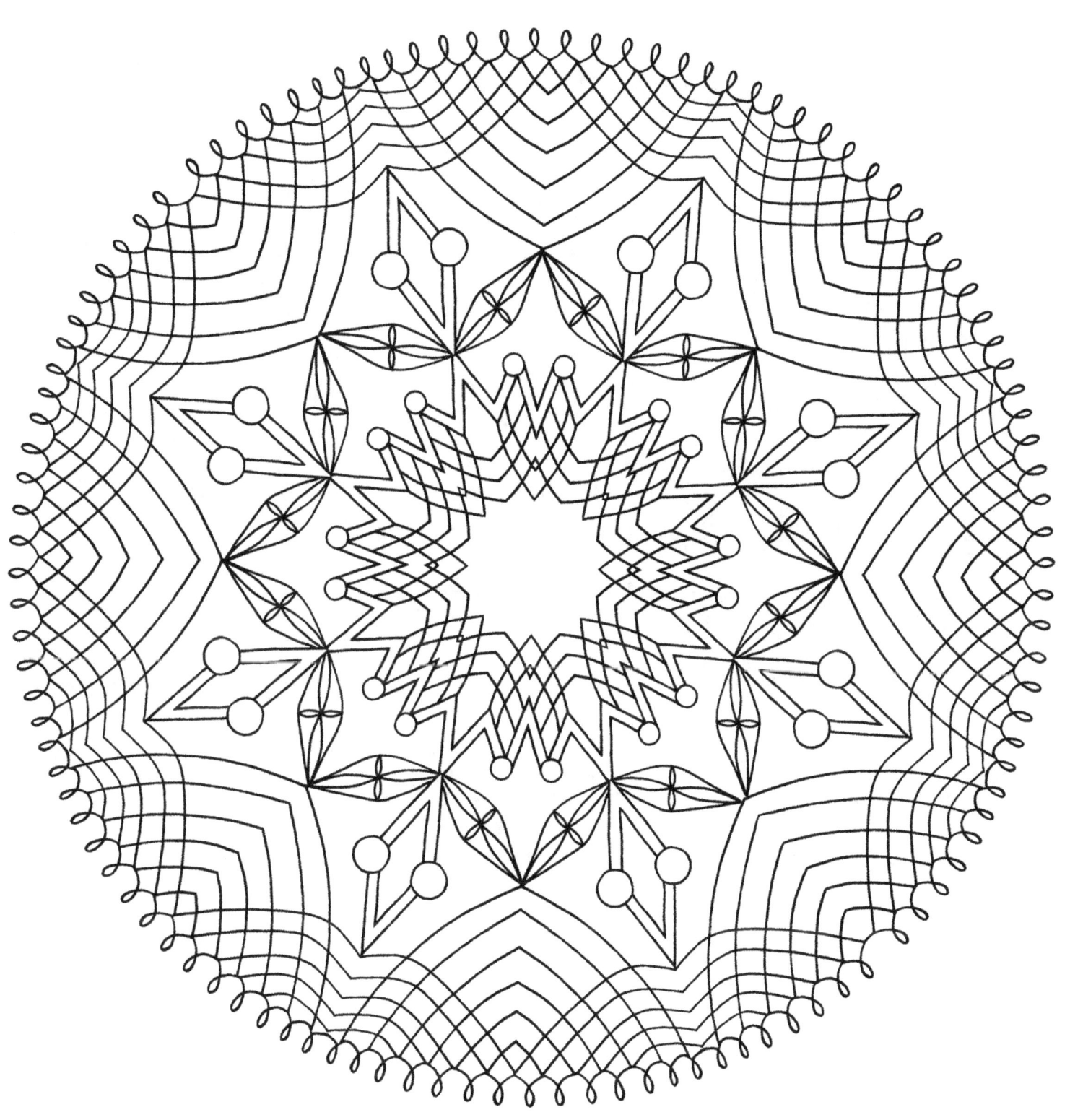

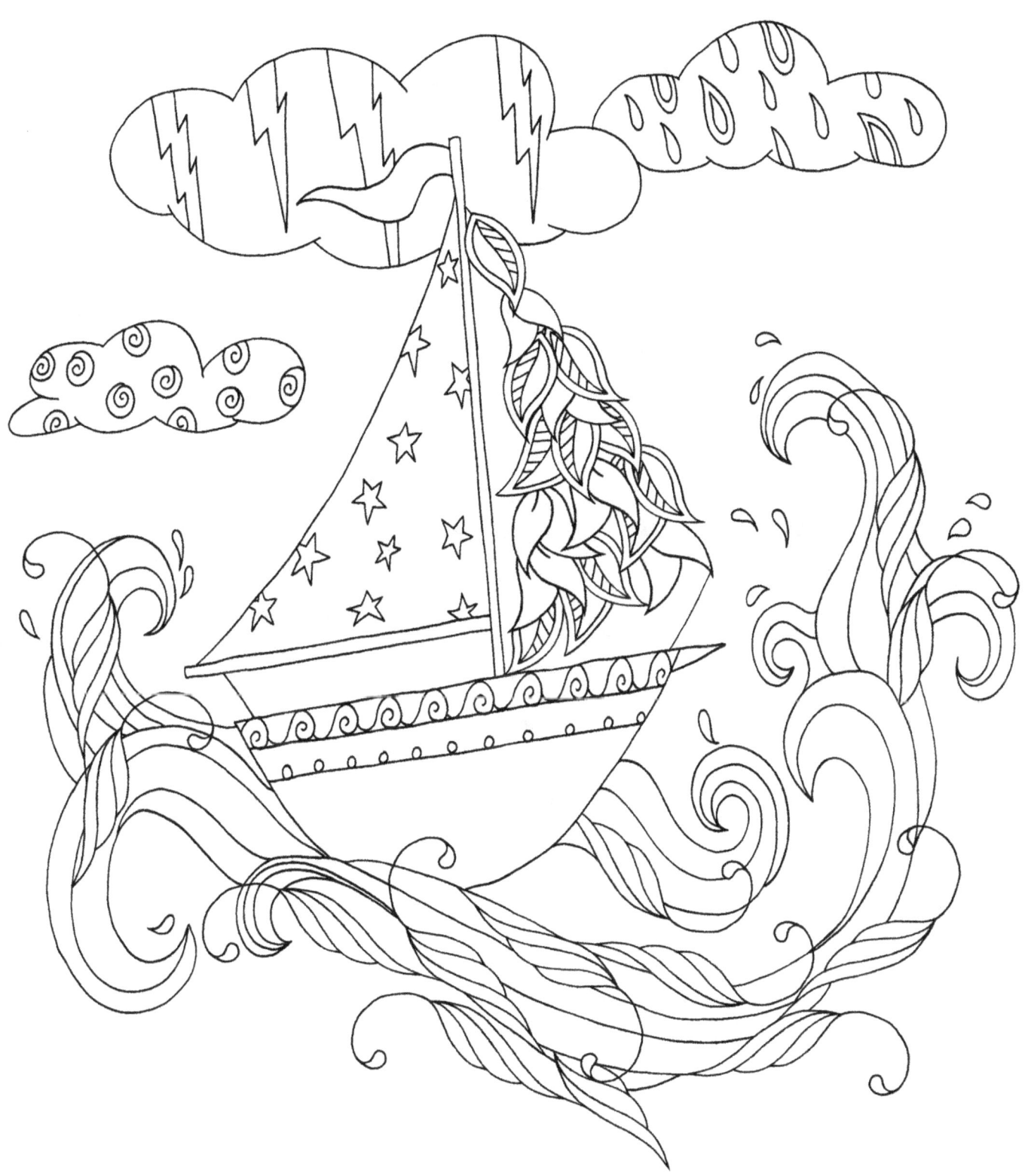

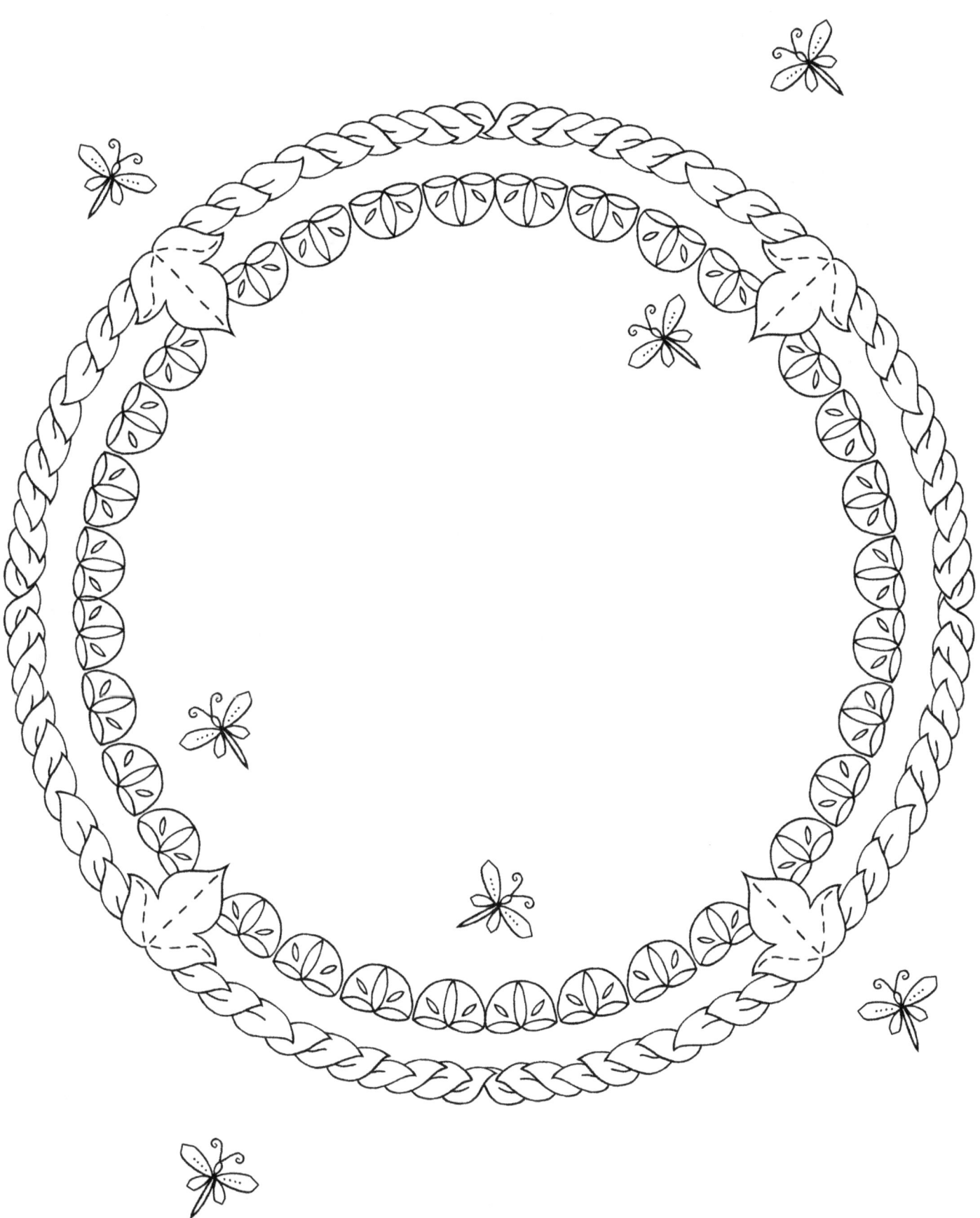

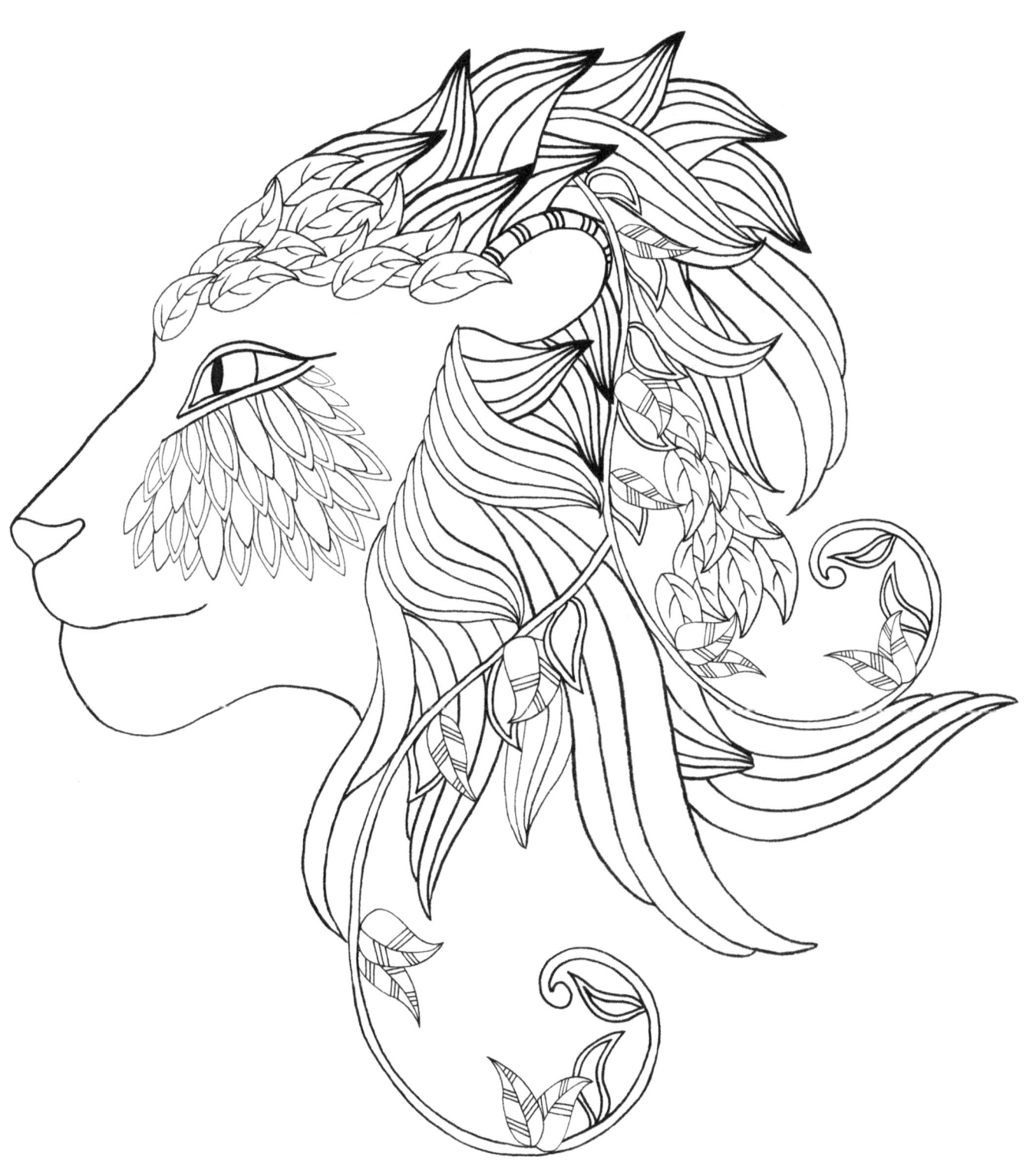

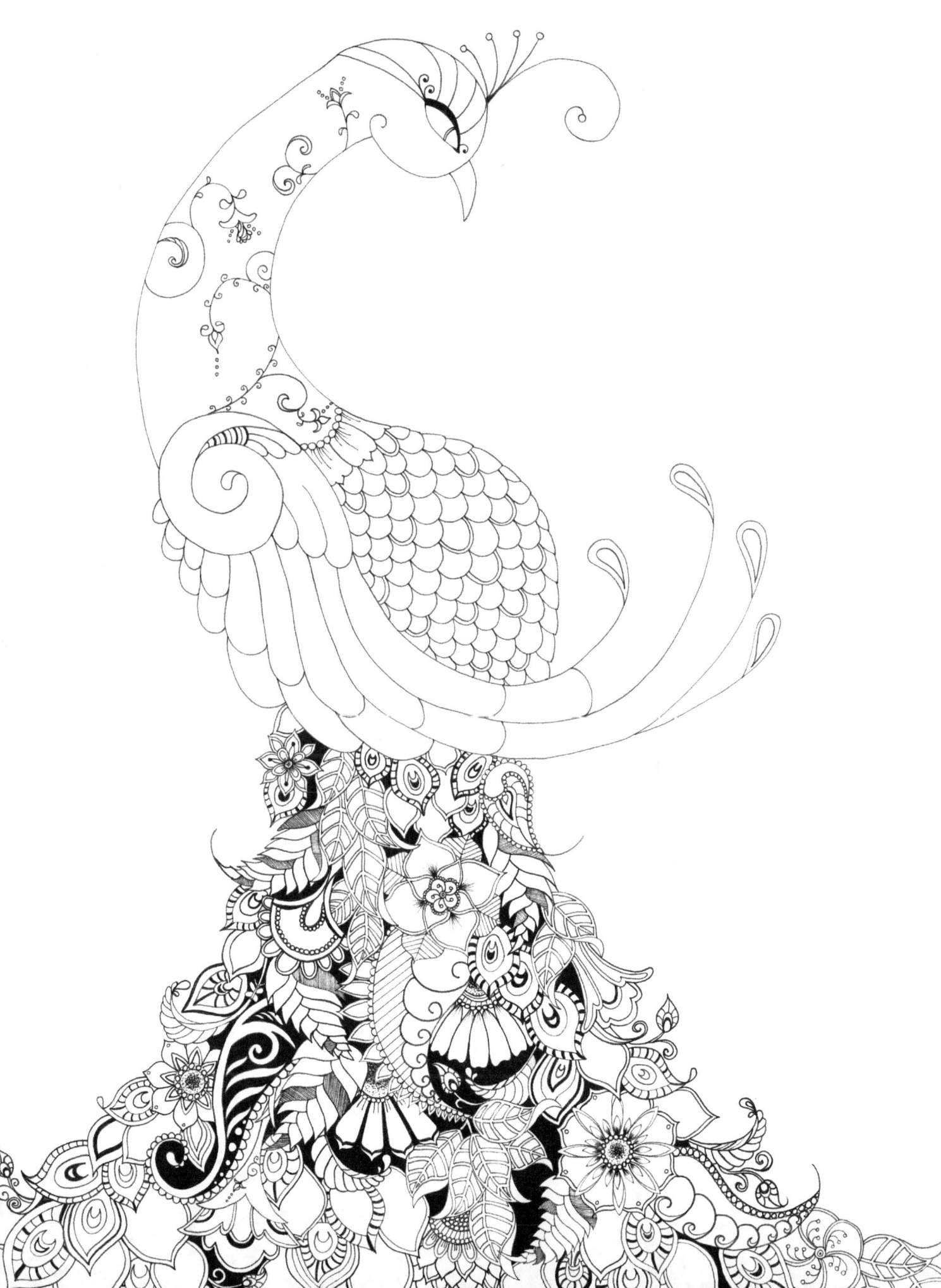

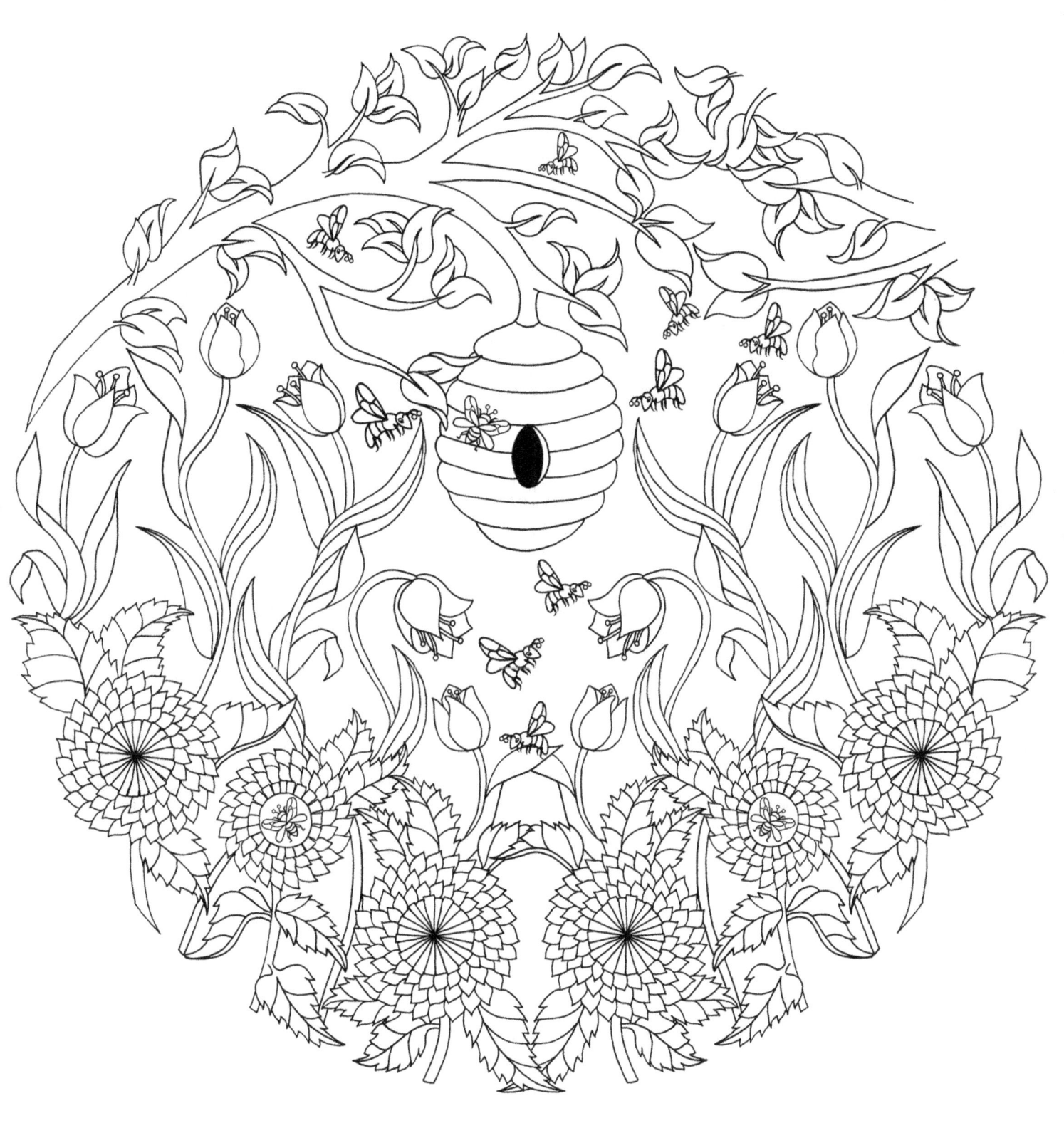

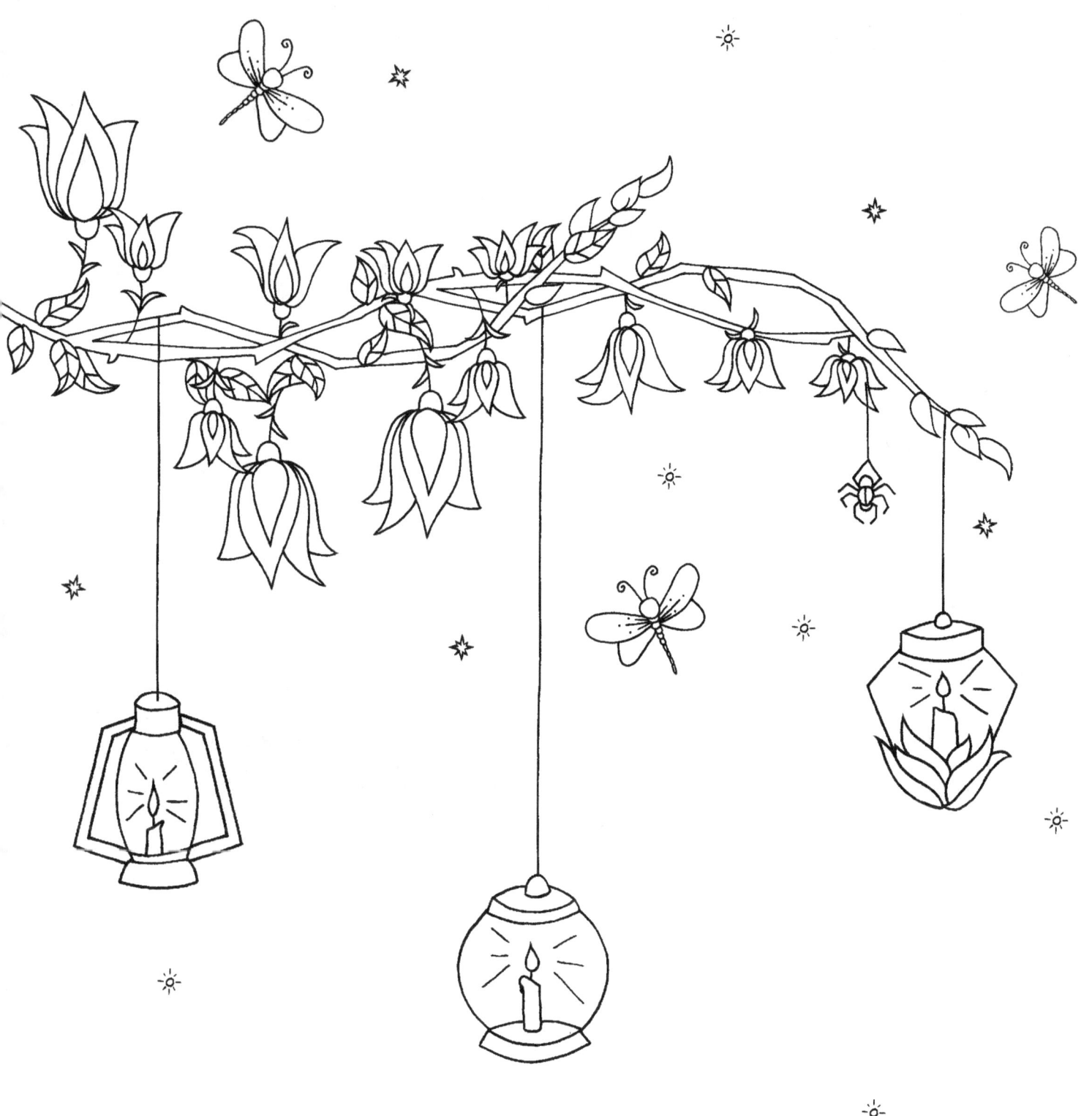

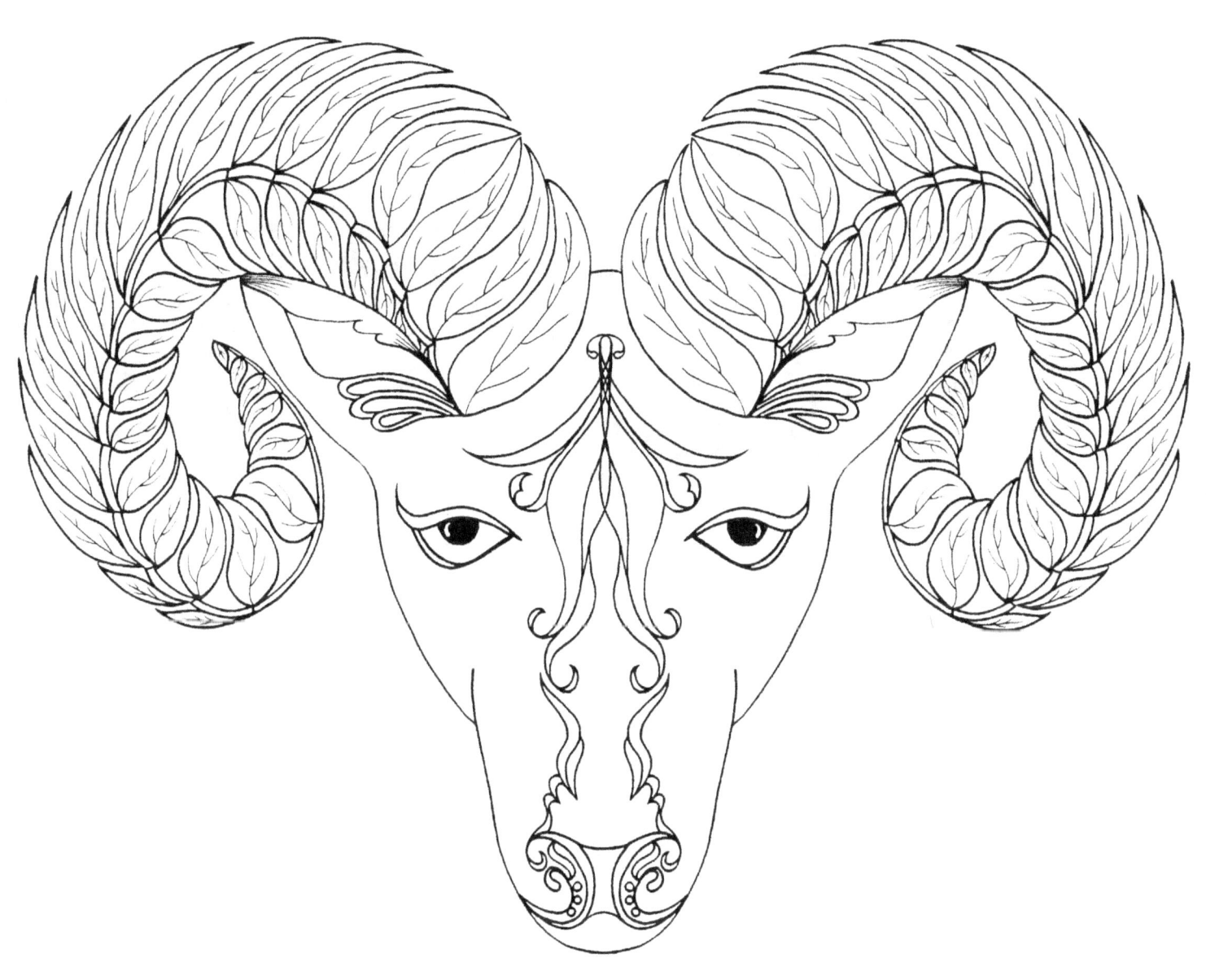

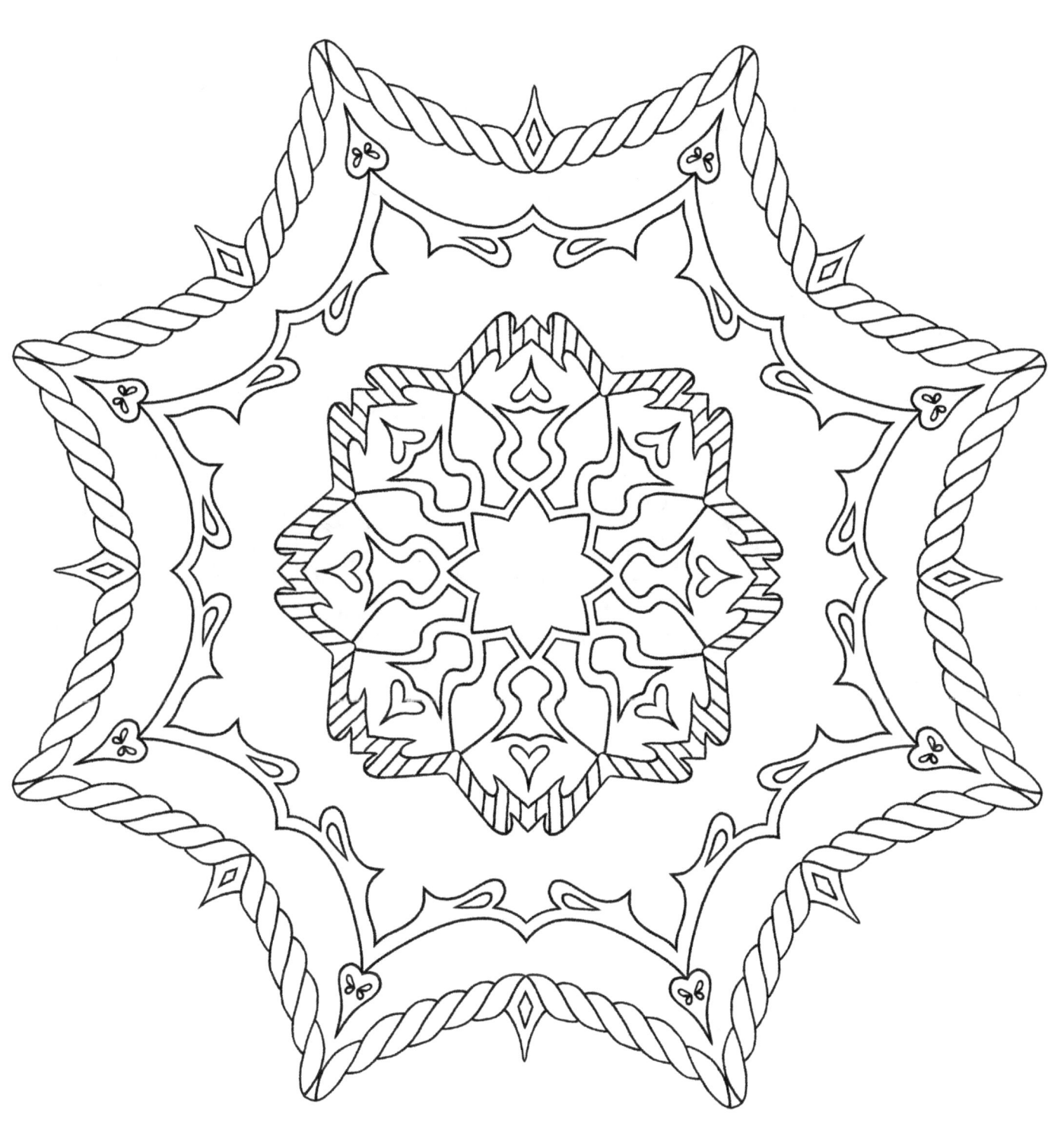

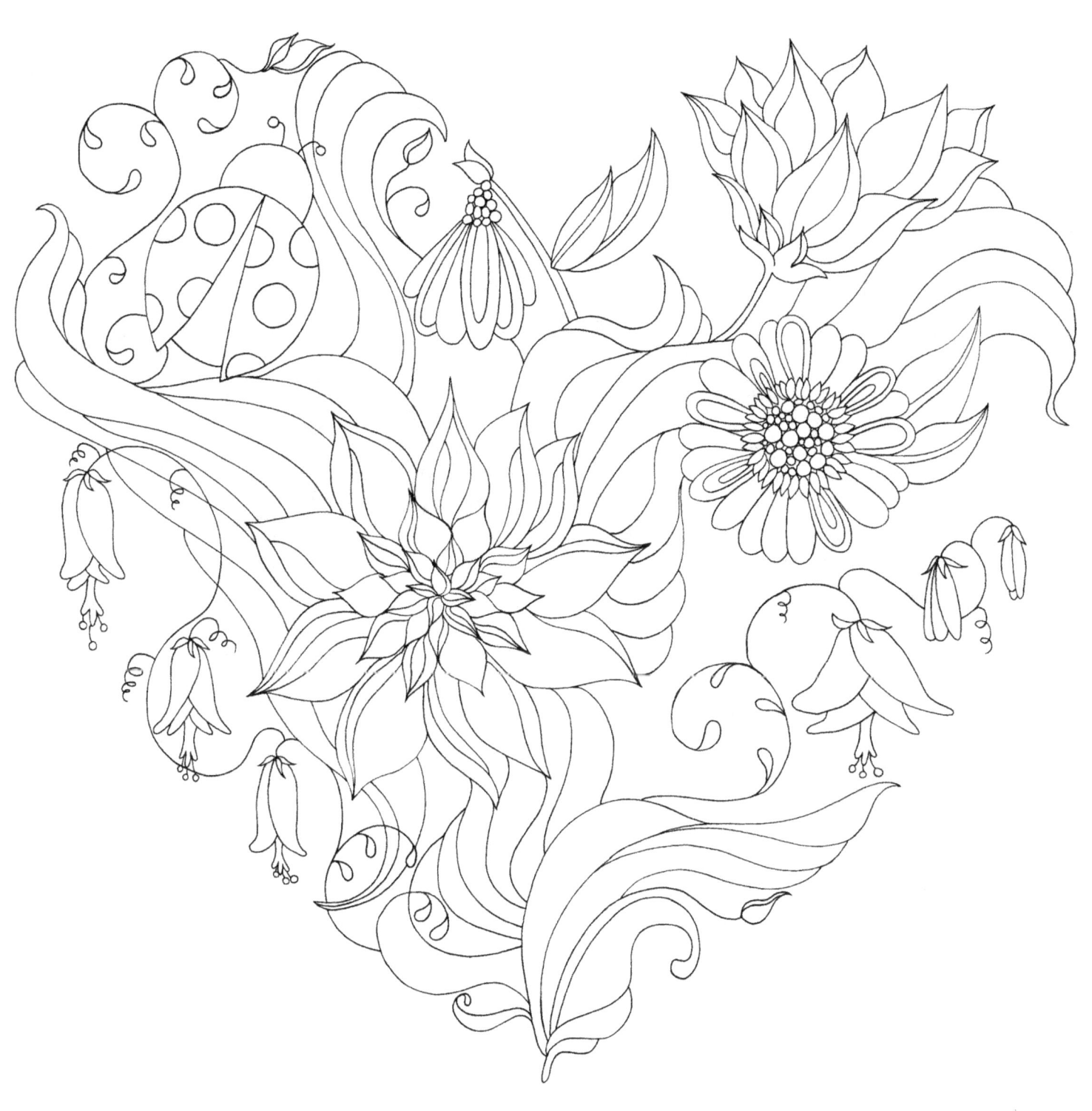

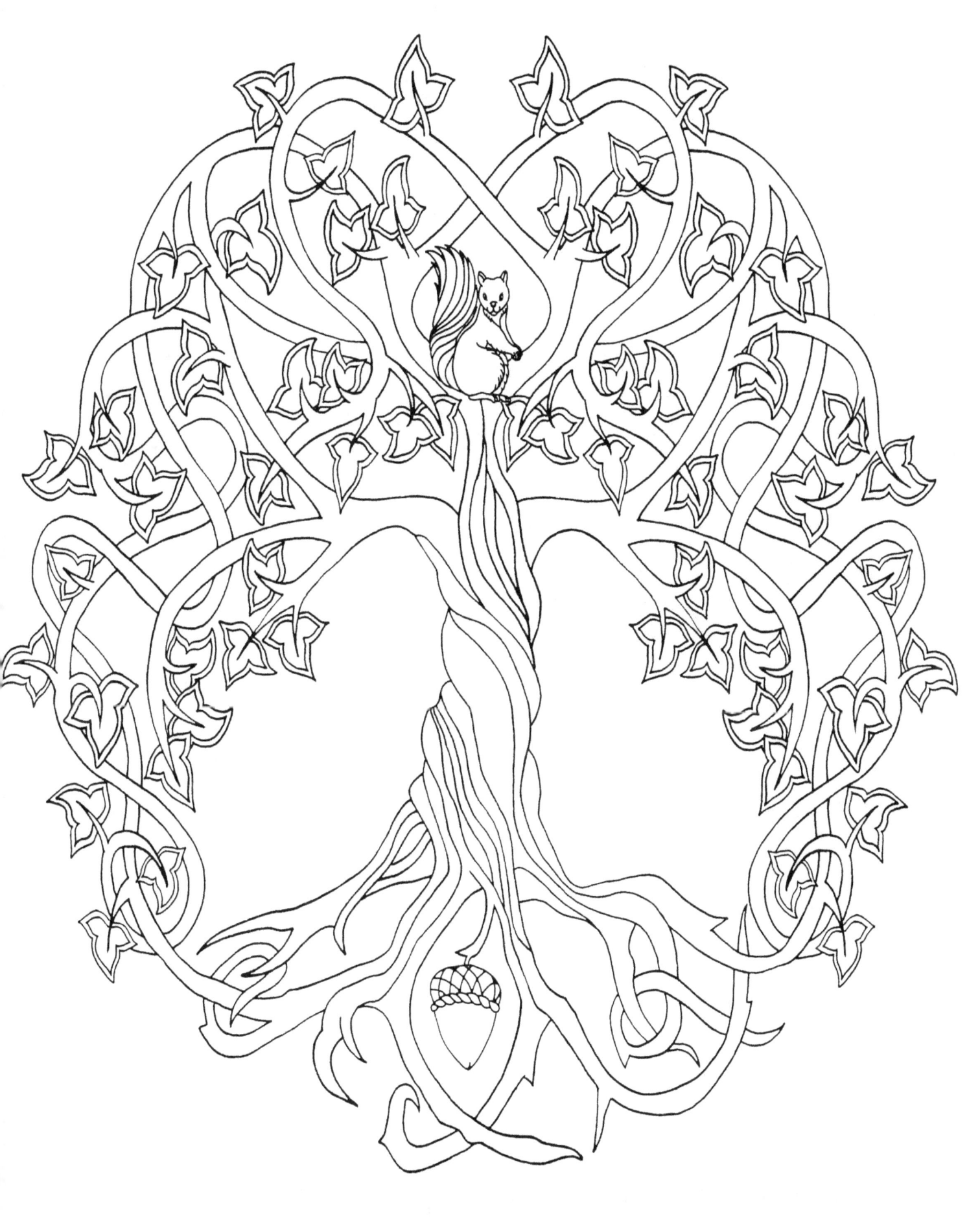

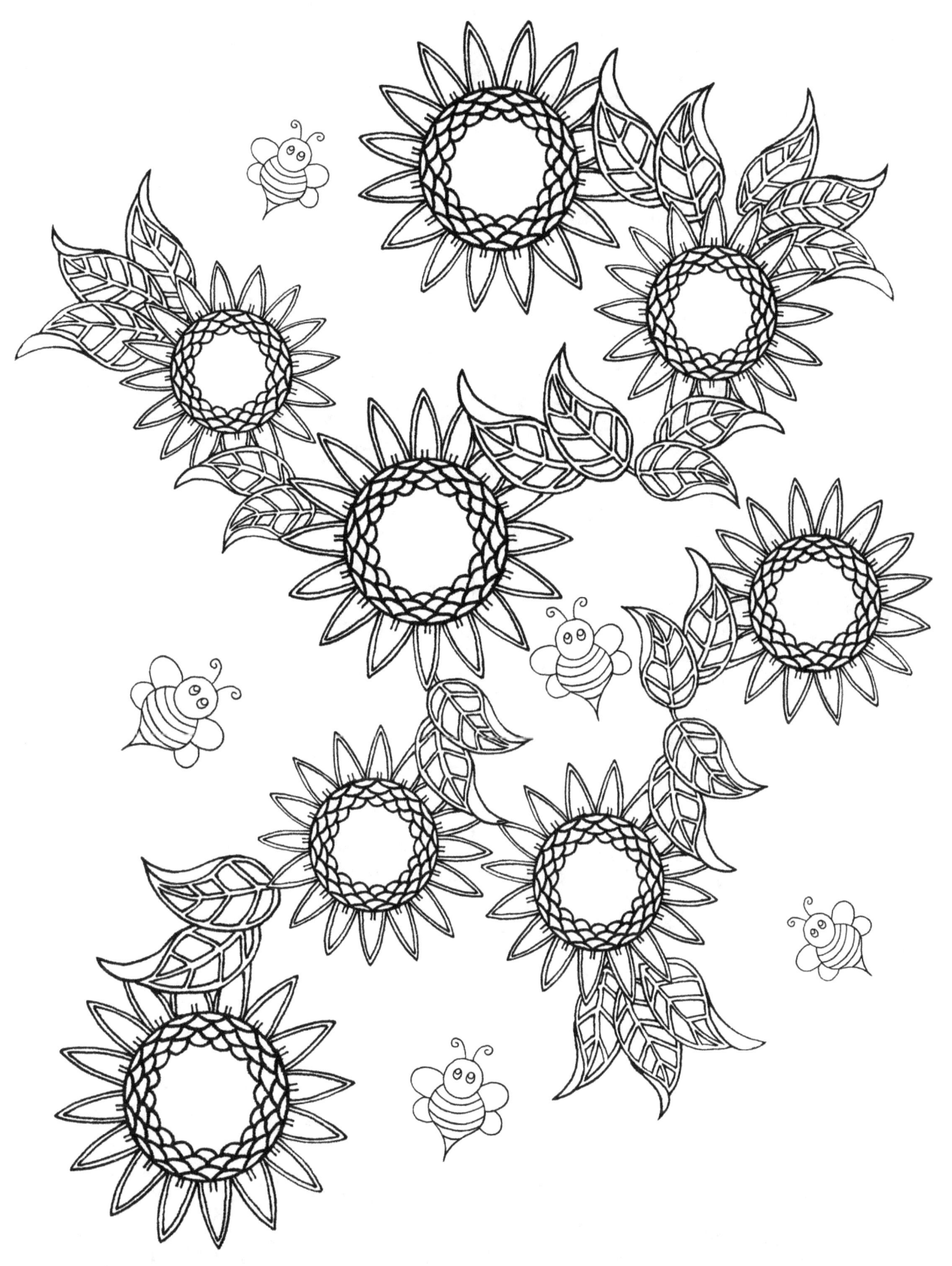

Color Palette Test Page

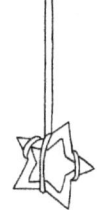

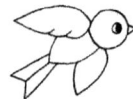

www.ingramcontent.com/pod-product-compliance
Lightning Source LLC
Chambersburg PA
CBHW082355220526
45470CB00008B/2752